COSBYOLOGY

COSBYOLOGY

essays and observations

from the doctor of comedy

BILL COSBY

WITH ORIGINAL ILLUSTRATIONS BY
GEORGE BOOTH

HYPERION
NEW YORK

Library of Congress Cataloging-in-Publication Data

Cosby, Bill.
    Cosbyology : essays and observations from the doctor of comedy
  by Bill Cosby.—1st ed.
        p.   cm.
    ISBN 0-7868-6810-4
    1. Cosby, Bill. 2. Comedians—United States—Biography. I. Title
    PN2287.C632   A3   2001
    792.7'028'092—dc21   2001016961

Book design by Casey Hampton

FIRST EDITION

10   9   8   7   6   5   4   3   2   1

TO JOHNNY BYRD (WALTER BYRD'S BROTHER),
who taught me how to dance

Contents

Introduction

A lot of writers—like Mark Twain and James Baldwin—write long books. And I have enjoyed those long books. But I have also enjoyed short stories. I have read short stories and had friends buy these short stories and my friends have enjoyed them. Short stories are stories. They have a beginning, a middle, and an end. And they are short. Short stories are the only short things you can make fun of and not get into trouble with short people.

The short stories that follow are good for giving you a respite from long Michener-type books. Everybody needs a break from an eight-hundred-page first chapter. When you finish an eight-hundred-page chapter one Michener or a nine-hundred-page introduction to a Michener classic on postage stamps, you want something to laugh at. Something you can hold in your hand that's not heavy. Something not written in a way that makes you feel like you've walked into the middle of a conversation. (Like the *New Yorker* magazine used to be.) You just want good, funny short stories.

And the other reason I love short stories is the opportunity to make up silly titles. No book could survive being called "Why I Don't Like Melting Snow Going Down the Crack of My Back" or "How You Can Chip Your Teeth *and* Pull a Ligament."

I hope you like this introduction because it's short.

I CAN DO MANY THINGS,
BUT I CANNOT WEAVE STRAW INTO LAUGHTER.

Oh, Baby!

PLANNING TO GET MARRIED SOON? Okay. Now listen to me carefully.

There was a song that spoke to me—thank God for melancholy poets and songwriters—because I couldn't express how badly I wanted her. But there was a song that said it all. And I just heard the words on the radio. "Ain't No Mountain High Enough."

Ain't no mountain high enough. To keep me from getting to you.

I mean, whether you're married or not, you know this song is telling your story. No mountain. High enough. To keep me from getting to you. Oh, baby. Oh, baby. No ocean wide enough to keep me from . . .

Oh, baby!

This beginning, this want, tells you to do things because you need that person. You accept this. And you will do things not asked of you by the person you want. As a matter of fact, you will volunteer. Like the song says.

You will climb mountains.

You will wade through rivers.

You will swim across oceans.

And the person you want hasn't even asked you to do anything like that. But you will do it.

The early years of marriage are fun—in retrospect—because both people are hoping it will last forever. Although they both would prefer to go straight to the Fiftieth Anniversary. That's because any sign of a difference in the relationship could cause "The Break Up." So, in the beginning, you will do anything to satisfy.

There will come a time in your marriage when both people begin to change. And, in that change, there will be things that you're not going to do for her anymore. And there will be things that she's not going to do for you anymore. Some of this may be happening now. You will notice that the person will just—boom—stop. And they're not doing that for you anymore. And don't forget what I said. It doesn't make any difference. There are things I'm not doing anymore. And not because I can't. Because I don't want to.

Let me give you an example of what I'm talking about.

Ain't no mountain high enough. To keep me from getting to you.

Oh, baby!

The first year, I would climb that mountain in the winter up eight thousand feet. All she had to do was call my name. I'm there. Eight thousand feet above Denver.

Oh, baby!

On a Monday night—during football season—I'm there! By her side. Asking her command.

Oh, baby!

And I don't know when the change occurred. I don't know if it was the fifth year or the fifteenth. But I know today if somebody came up to me and said: Mr. Cosby, your wife is up on the top of the mountain and said for you to come up and get her. First thing I'd say is: Well, what the hell is she doing up there? Then I'd call my daughter and say: Go up there and get your mother and bring her down here and take her over to the hospital and see if she's all right.

Oh, baby!

But I love her more today than back then.

In the first years of your marriage you have to go to the bathroom, see. So you get up and you take your wife's arms—the two of you have been just holding each other, you know, you hold each other like you're floating. And suddenly, you hear this booming voice in your head.

You better go to the bathroom!

So you hit the light. *Click!* And she sits up and she's startled and she says: "Oh, what's the matter, honey?"

You turn around and you kiss her—kiss, kiss, kiss—and say: "Nothing wrong, dear. Nothing wrong."

And she holds you.

"Oh, it startled me. The lights were going on."

And you say: "Yes, darling, but I'll be all right. I'll be all right."

"You're not leaving me are you?"

And you reassure her.

"No, honey. No."

And you kiss, and then you kiss some more. And you reassure her some more, tell her that everything is fine.

"I was just so frightened," she explains. "Where are you going?"

"Honey, I'm going to the bathroom, that's all."

And you kiss and you back away looking at her. And she's got her arm out. And you walk around the bed and you say: "I'll be back, I'll be back."

And she says: "I'll miss you."

And then you make another dash to hold her on the other side of the bed.

"It won't be long, darling. It won't be long."

And you go to the bathroom and you hurry yourself. You hurry and you clean up and you come back and she's still sitting there with her arms out.

"I thought you'd gone and left me," she says, sounding so relieved.

"No, honey, my darling."

And you kiss her and you turn the lights out and it's just fantastic. You know?

And I don't know if it was the fifth year or the fifteenth.

But it was the most frightening experience and since then I haven't turned on those lights. I had to go to the bathroom—and as you get older you have to go, and sometimes by the time you get there you wonder why you got up. But I had to go. The booming voice told me I had to go.

You better get out of this bed!

And so I reached over and I hit the lights. *Click!* And a voice came out from my wife's body—I swear, I had never heard it before—and I jumped back and I said: "What?"

And this scary voice said something unintelligible. And I started to back away because I was frightened. I didn't know if this was some demon from *The Exorcist* in a high voice or what. And the face, her face was horrible—it was an angry face—but I knew it wasn't my wife.

So I said: "Who are you? Speak!"

And she spoke. It sounded like a high-pitched howling into a strong, whistling wind.

"Turn off the liiighgh!"

I couldn't make out the words so I asked: "The what?"

"The light! The light!"

"What is wrong with it?"

She shrieked: "Turn the light out!"

"But dear," I said calmly, "I have to go to the—"

The voice screamed back at me. "I don't care!"

And then she went into like a chant or something.

"Turn the light out. Turn the light out. Turn the light out. Turn the light out."

It was frightening. And then she grabbed the covers, pulled them over her head, *whoosh*, and from under the covers the voice kept chanting: "Turn the light out. Turn the light out. Turn the light out. Turn the light out."

And so I turned the lights out and it didn't get any better. The voice was even scarier.

"Turn the light out! Light! Out! Out! Light!"

And I found myself walking to the bathroom in the dark and not knowing where I was. And so I went into the bathroom. Which brings me to a thought.

You know, when you go into the bathroom in the middle of the night, you do the dumbest things. You gamble and you don't touch the light at all. Walking in the dark, half asleep, searching for the bowl. And you find it with your calves. And you really think you're a genius. Yeah! You find the bowl with your calves. The calves will tell you because it's nice and cold around the bowl there.

Feeling . . . feeling . . . okay! There it is! Easy. All right, we're on the right side of the bowl. Got it? All right, now we go the other way. So now you know you're straddling the bowl. I'm talking about men now. You know you're over the bowl. Now, you make a decision. You think: Should we gamble on if it's up or down? So, depending upon how long ago you were burned, you reach down and you say: "Oh, boy! I'm glad we didn't go for that shot that time!"

You lift up the lid and then you lift up the seat. You can't see, so you put your hand out and you lean against the wall and you rest your head on your shoulder. You're going to take a nap while you're going to the bathroom. Now, for men, you listen to the sound to tell you where you are. And that's the dumbest thing. Because you hear a high pitch and you say: "Are we on there or what?"

Now the stupid part is that when you start to move in the dark then you hear: *Brong!*

You know you're on it now. And you have this conversation in your head.

Okay, now go to sleep. Go to sleep. But we made a mess. Yeah, we're going to have to clean it up. But right now I'm going to take a nap.

I'm going to tell you women something about men. Something that no man will tell you. It doesn't make any difference how much money, how big, how tall, how old, whatever, we all do the same thing. You're in a public place and you go to the men's room and you step up to the urinal and you are ready. The first thrust hits.

Whoosh!

And, of course, you're looking down. And you see, flying around in this bowl, a little black bug. And the thing is, it's not leaving the bowl, it's just flying around. You decide to declare war on this bug. This is really a great video game. I wish you women could see it because there are literally hundreds of men standing and dipping and bobbing and that's why they have those stalls there because men have literally followed the bug and hit another man.

"Hey, man! Keep your game over there to yourself!"

But I have never killed or drowned one of these bugs and you always get mad at yourself for running out of ammunition. And that's why you see men come out of the men's room angry. Go right up to the bar and growl at the bartender.

"Give me nine bottles of beer. Right now! Nine bottles of beer because I'm going to kill a bug."

And the bartender says: "Oh, you got a tough one in there in stall three, George."

I want all of you to pay attention to this—those of you getting married soon. There's a sleeping position, greatest position of all time. It didn't happen until I got married and so I want to explain this to people who are getting married. The fellow, you get into bed and you're in this position—on your side, curled up—and you wait for your mate, and she's in the bathroom—you're in this curled position on your side—and she comes out of the bathroom, turns the light out, and gets in the bed. She backs in.

Oh, baby!

And you slide your left arm under her left arm and you pull her in even closer. There's no air between the two of you.

Oh, baby!

Your knees are bent, her knees are bent, I mean, the two of you, it's just fantastic. And you put your lips out softly and you say "Goodnight, dear." And she turns around and your lips meet and you kiss.

Oh, baby!

So you finish a wonderful kiss and it's the beginning, the first year of your marriage. Then comes that part that I didn't know about that makes it, it just makes it. You take your leg and you put it on top of her, just over her left hip. You just drop it right there, bent. And she'll even reach down and grab it.

Oh, baby!

And that is the best position, it's better than sucking your thumb. I mean, and you keep that leg on her. She can turn over this way, you keep that leg right on her. And she'll move, you just follow her. You just stay right on her man, no matter where she goes you keep that leg on her.

Oh, baby!

It is the most wonderful thing. And I said: "God bless marriage. I didn't know anything about this. Fantastic!"

And I don't know if it was the fifth year or the fifteenth. I know she came out of the bathroom and she had on these killer curlers and I had on my hockey goalie mask. And she turned the light out and she got in the bed and backed in.

Boom!

And she knocked the wind out of me.

Oh, baby!

I kissed her on the shoulder and she kissed straight ahead. I put my leg on top of her. All of a sudden I heard a whistle. She said: "Wheeeet!"

And she grabbed my leg and threw it.

"Hey! Take that leg off of me! Nobody wants a big fat leg hanging on them the rest of their life. Cutting off my circulation. What do you think I am, a pack mule? How would you like it if I put my leg on you?"

But I love her more today—more today—than back then.

Oh, baby!

Look, I'm telling you it's so cute the first year. The first year of our marriage she would get up in the morning to get ready for the day. It was so cute. And she would go into the bathroom and she was so quiet. You didn't hear any water running or anything. She was just tiptoeing around. And I always felt she was doing that because she didn't want me to hear her in there getting ready. Which I thought was cute. First year of marriage.

Oh, baby!

She thought I would leave her if I heard her in there, you know. Fantastic! And she'd come out an hour later just looking beautiful, man.

Oh, baby!

And I don't know if it was the fifth year or the fifteenth.

I really don't know. I know that she got out of the bed and I heard the door close.

Slam!

And the water.

Pshhh!

And she gargled.

Rbarbarbarba!

Oh, boy. All right. That was the one we were trying to get.

And then she came out an hour later looking the same as when she went in there. But I love her more today than back then when she was quiet.

Oh, baby!

There was a time in the beginning of our marriage I'd be sleeping. Snoring. And she said: "Bill. Bill. Honey, you're snoring. Roll over on your stomach, I'll rub your back."

Oh, baby!

And I don't know if it was the fifth year or the fifteenth. I know I was asleep. And all of a sudden, panic set in my body and I knew I was dying. But there was a panic there because I knew there was no oxygen in my body. And I tried to open my mouth but I couldn't because my lips somehow were Scotch-taped together. And I tried to breathe through my nose and I opened my eyes and my wife was on top of me stuffing cotton in my nose. And she had a look on her face.

"I'm sick of this! I haven't slept in five weeks. All night that's all I've heard."

But I love her more today than back then when she would let me live.

Oh, baby!

Why I Don't Like Melting Snow Going Down the Crack of My Back

I HAVE A FRIEND OF MINE who has been divorced three times. So, this friend of mine, who—at the time I was in my for- ties—he's fifty-something, says: "Cos. I want you to go ski- ing with me."

"Really," I said. "I don't want to go skiing."

"Look," he insisted. "You have not experienced the feeling of going downhill with the wind in your face and the sound and the freedom of going down at this speed and it's just you and God."

And he started to rhapsodize. And I kept looking at him and I kept saying: "Wonderful! For you. But I don't want to."

Well, he's one of these people, they keep it up and they keep it up. Finally I said: "Okay, I'll go with you. I'll go with you on a Saturday."

"Oh! Great!"

So he came over on Saturday and said: "I'll take you over to the store to buy the stuff."

Okay. So we go over to this place, all these salespeople walking around with a tan, wrinkled skin but white circles around their eyes. They looked like negatives of raccoons. And they all have great, white teeth. Healthy-looking teeth.

So the salesguy said: "Okay. Why don't you sit down and we'll measure your foot and get you into a boot."

So I said to the fellow: "Do me a favor. I don't want the most expensive, I want the best."

"No problem. You sit down and you take off the shoes and the socks."

"Okay."

And then he brought a basket with some used sweat socks in them. Well, there's a certain thing about used sweat socks. I think I could use some stranger's toothbrush and it would not bother me as much as somebody else's sock.

My toes drew back—this guy had never seen anything like it. You know how a turtle's head goes in—all of my toes went way back into the foot.

"I've never seen this before," he said.

"They don't want a used sock," I said. "Now, if you get a pack of fresh sweat socks, these toes will come back out."

So he brought out fresh socks, and I put them on and he measured my foot. So then the fellow comes back with a box of ski boots.

"All right," he instructed, "just put your foot in."

Well, I'm not used to going in—these blue things looked like two shiny cinder blocks. So I go in sideways with the foot, turn, push.

"Now," he said. "Just push hard and bang your heel."

And now I'm going *bang, bang, bang*. And then *cushh!* I'm in. This is how you put a ski boot on. So he fastened the things. *Clong, clong clong. Plong*. And now my ankle is locked. So he did the same thing with the other foot. Locked ankles!

Now what these boots have done is that they've taken away my ankles. I mean, there's nothing that moves now except my knees. I have no ankles. This friend of mine tells me that skiing, you get in touch with God and the ski boot just took away what God gave me. Ankles!

"Okay," the guy said. "Stand up."

"Look," I pointed out, "you just locked my ankles."

"Go ahead," he urged me. "Stand up."

I kept my knees bent because if I straightened my legs out I knew I was going to fall. Because I needed my ankles.

"Rock to the left," he told me.

And I went to my left.

And then he said: "Rock to the right."

And I went to my right.

And he said: "Now make a circle."

And I did like, I made a circle. But I was beginning to feel what he was talking about, you know. And I began to see myself out there. And I began to see snow slicing—I was slicing snow left and right and oh, boy, I was feeling. And I didn't even have poles yet.

"Now walk," he said.

And that was when it got funny because I had no ankles.

"Now walk a little bit more and rock a little bit more."

And I loved that part. And then I backed up and he said: "Sit down."

"Okay."

"How do they feel?"

"I'm glad you asked," I said. "Now right here on this right foot, right here in the middle of the foot, there's a bone and the shoe is pressing this bone and it is really, it is hurting, man. It is painful. Right there it's mashing that bone. But up top here where the boot starts, that's rubbing on my skin and it is making it raw. Raw! Starting there. Now, on the other side of my foot, where the big toe is, well there's a bone there and it's mashing that bone. And underneath, where my arch is, there's a blister coming up here."

I took a breath and continued.

"Now the other foot. My little toe—I don't know what happened—but when I stamped down, my little toe got mixed up and it's somewhere under my big toe. The other three toes in the middle are really confused, they're all on top of each other. And there is a cut, I think it's bleeding now, I don't know, because I can't feel anything because this other bone cut the nerve. So everything is numb, but up top here this is bleeding right away."

"Great," he said. "They fit."

Now, I was walking around this place buying stuff, man. I was caught! You had to have two outfits. One was for your skin and the other was to cover up that part. So I bought these skintight things, and they keep the heat of your own body in but don't let cold into your body. You understand what I'm saying? So then you put on these other pants and they block the cold from getting to the part that wouldn't let the cold in anyway. So you are insulated with your own body heat. So you will never get cold. These things are tight. And I put a top on and that was tight. And a jacket. So that cost $1,700, you know. But it wasn't the most expensive. It was the best.

I bought some sunglasses—cost $600—that will never let the sun in. As a matter of fact, you can't see. But everybody said I looked cool. People said: "You don't even look like you're looking at me."

"I'm not," I said.

And I bought some poles for the skis. They cost $700 because they're special—they won't leave your hand. And I bought some gloves—Day-Glo—so that if I'm skiing in the street cars can see me when I'm coming. And I paid $3,500 for the skis because these are new skis—you never have to wax them, they wax themselves. There's a little motor on the side waxing.

So I come out and we're going skiing and my friend asked me: "Are you happy?"

"Yeah," I said. "But I don't know anything about skiing."

He helped me put the skis on top of his car. He's got this little thing now. So he started the car and it went: *putter, putter, putter.* But you know what I've noticed about little cars like that? The heater. We're talking perseverance, man. We're talking about a heater!

I've got these clothes on that already I'm 98.6. I mean, sweat was rolling off of me and staying within me. And he's got this heater, this little tube, and this thing was kicking off, it was about 105 and you can't turn the thing off. If you do, the engine will shut down. And I was sitting there and this guy was driving and sweat was running down my face. I've got about five pounds of sweat splashing in the seat of my pants and it won't go anywhere, it's just sitting and I'm beginning to feel like a balloon, you know, a water balloon. So I said: "You know that guy should have sold this to me with a little spigot so that when it gets too much I could let it out. What is it? It's just sweat, don't bother me."

But I do know there's one thing that will break your concentration. I don't care what you're doing and how good it is. If a trickle of sweat runs down the middle of your back, that will get your attention because you know where it's headed. Ah, what are you doing? And the thing just kept going down and all this water is hanging there. So, I've got on these sunglasses where nobody can tell whether I'm looking. I had the window rolled down, I was hanging, you know, trying to live, man, 'cause I was cooking myself in my own juices. And people were driving past and everybody's passing us 'cause this car is going: *prrrrr*.

I'm going to tell you and you're not going to believe me, but I don't care. I don't care. But I'm going to tell you what I saw. And it happened. This car was going along— *prrrrr*—and my friend shifted into third and the car said: *prrr, prrr, prrrrr*. And then it took a breath. Now I knew you wouldn't believe me but I don't care. I don't care. The car said: *ahhhh*.

So we were driving and he pulls into a parking lot.

"Well," he said. "We're here."

So I look to see where the people are skiing.

"Where are the people skiing?"

"Oh," he said. "We have to walk a mile."

I frowned.

"In these boots?"

I didn't want the guy to think, well, Bill started with a bad attitude. I wanted him to feel that when I say I don't like skiing he's going to understand that I gave it a great shot. So I said: "Well, here we go!"

Those of you who have never skied before, let me tell you now. You see these movies of people and they're smiling and they look happy and everything? It's cold up there. It is cold up there.

I got out of the car and I was sweating, see, from the heater, and I've got about, now ten pounds. And it was just sitting in the seat of my pants. It won't move. Because the other stuff was so tight, I've got a water bag, and I've got ten pounds of my own body juices. And the wind hit me. *Whoosh!* And it froze the water bag and my face. So I was smiling when I got out of the car and my face was frozen. I spoke. I wasn't talking to anyone in particular. But when the words came out, I discovered I had developed an accent.

"Oh my God! It's cold!"

And I heard myself talking with this accent.

"Oh my God! It's sort of cold up here."

The more I heard myself the more I realized I was sounding German. And then it dawned on me—I see all these movies and people are talking, and they are sounding German. But now I know that they are not German. Their faces are frozen, and this is why they talk like that. So my friend, he got out of the car, and he was smiling and it froze his face too. So I said: "Ha, ha! Your face is frozen!"

And he said: *"Javohl, mein Herr!"*

So, we took the skis and we were walking. In these boots. And with the frozen sweat in the seat of the pants. And I walked a mile with my friend and my face was frozen. And then we got to the place and there was a line of people—about seven thousand. So we got behind them. And we were moving one foot every three days. I was standing in line and my feet—I don't know what color they were now—but I was afraid they were going to be cut off. It was just pitiful. My thighs were cramping because they had stayed bent for so long. And there was about forty pounds of ice in the seat of my pants. And my face was frozen. And now my nose started to run. I'm a forty-year-old man. And my nose was running. I had cramps in my legs. And I turned to my friend and I said: "You know, I'm having the most fun. I don't see how I could enjoy myself just being home eating potato chips watching TV. This is far more fun than I've ever had in my life. And I want to thank you for taking me here."

And I had the skis on my shoulder and on purpose I turned around quickly. And hit him right in the face. And it was so cold, he didn't bleed. And I looked and his nose was running too.

And so now we were moving and I'm having so much fun I don't know what to do. Finally we get to the point where the chair comes. This is the rudest thing on the face of this earth. Because if it misses, it's going to take your head off. It's gone. You'll hear: *Boom!* That's it. And there you are frozen and it's so cold you don't even bleed. You just stand there.

And so finally the thing came and—*boom*—I'm in the chair, I've got the skis on, I'm holding on. Thank God for the forty-pound bag of ice. Because that was what kept me from falling off the thing. And I was holding on to this and I didn't want anybody to know that I was scared. So I just said to myself: *Mein, God!* I'm going to die!

So the chair took me up: 2,800 feet closer to God. I saw people going into Heaven. That's how high up I was. I was holding on trying not to fall.

The chair came down to where I was supposed to jump off. Now these idiots who made the place, they didn't make it like a carpet or something so you could get off. You start skiing right away. So I was supposed to jump off, but I can't jump off because there were people on the ground—there were people on the ground! And they were screaming.

"Please don't. Please don't jump on us, mister! Please! My God! Please don't jump on us! Please!"

"But I'm supposed to jump off. Why don't you—"

"No! Please! For God's sake, don't do that! Don't do that!"

So I had to take the chair on back around again. Now, the next time I came back there were not as many people on the ground. There was a little opening. So I jumped off and I started skiing right away. And I was moving. And so I did a little jerking. And I remembered from a film I had seen: point your toes in, you won't go as fast. So then I took my toes and I put them underneath. I don't know how fast I was going, but it wasn't anything like what my friend had described yet. So I figured—maybe a little faster I will meet God and all of that. But at the moment it was just sort of going. But then my right foot started to angle away from my body. I said to the left one: "Follow him! Don't let him get away from you, home." And I was doing pretty good, I was picking up speed. And I wasn't afraid.

Now, those of you who've never skied before, listen to me carefully. Keep your feet parallel. Straight ahead. Don't worry about going too fast. Be your own judge of how fast you want to go. If you start to go too fast, don't panic. Take your poles and stick 'em forward. And you will stop.

So I was going, you know, and got up to maybe fifteen miles an hour. I was cooking, man. But I noticed that there were skiers all over this place who really—I don't know how to describe them—but they free-form. After you get going, you can do whatever you want. And 80 percent of the skiers I saw were going sixty, fifty miles an hour. And they didn't know how to ski. Yeah, the fastest skiers don't know how to ski. But they free-form. And they're not on their skis. No. They're on the ground. There was one guy who went backward. Downhill. And at the bottom of the hill went around like he meant to do it. Then there was a guy who hit a tree and called the tree stupid.

"Ah, the stupid tree was in the way."

So I'm skiing and all of a sudden this woman came at me. Forty miles an hour. She screamed at me.

"Get out of the way!"

And I didn't know what to do. But she was coming at me, you know, and I tried to veer—I didn't know what the Hell I was doing. She hit me.

Boom!

I went up in the air and came down.

Boom!

On top of her.

Nice-looking lady. But her nose was running.

The Day I Found Out How the Projects Were Built

I WAS SIX YEARS OLD. And at six, it was a beautiful life. I played. I ate snacks. I listened to the radio a lot. And there were these voices on the radio constantly coming at me.

"Buy this! Buy that! Do this! Do that!"

If you're close to my age, you probably remember Gabby Hayes had a radio program and there was a ring that you could get with a box of something and twenty-five cents. And this ring had a cannon on the end. But you didn't have to have a driver's license or anything to get this ring—you could be four years old—and you could just send for it. *Boom!* You could shoot your finger off!

Now, when I was six, there was a program—I'm going to sound like old people now because I don't remember what the man was selling—but there was this program on the radio and whatever it was they were selling cost fifteen cents. Of course, it wasn't just fifteen cents. You also had to send in the top from a box of Kix cereal. (My parents always bought Corn Flakes, which very seldom had anything to send away for. I think there was a napkin or something to wipe your mouth that you could send away for but that was about it for the Corn Flakes.)

Anyway, this thing I wanted that cost fifteen cents and a box top from Kix—I don't remember what it was but I remember the man said I had to have it and it sounded good.

"Kids! You *have* to have it!"

He said: "Kids!" And that was me! And he said: "Go tell your mom and dad. Get a box of Kix and you send a box top to . . ."

I'm not sure but I think it was Battle Creek, Michigan. You send a box top from Kix and fifteen cents to Battle Creek, Michigan, and you get this wonderful thing. I mean. What is fifteen cents? Nothing.

My parents—we lived in the Richard Allen Housing Projects—my parents were not poor, they were broke. There's a difference. Broke people are no fun to live with because, wherein the guy on the radio kept saying I had to have it, my broke parents kept saying: "We don't have it."

And they just kept on saying "We don't have it," and I couldn't understand that. Not only could I not understand it, I refused to accept it.

But I had to be careful because old people were armed in those days. You didn't know what they were going to do to you or even what they *could* do to you. You just knew they could do *something*, and after that you wouldn't be around. So you could never push your parents to where they would get angry enough to become violent.

You know those dogs with the mushed faces and the wrinkles all around them? My father told me if I ever did something to him again—like embarrass him in public, because I yelled at him in public once—he would make me look like one of those dogs. And I remember my mother saying she would knock me into the middle of next week. And there were times when I really wanted to go there because that would give me at least four days away from them. I figured I could wait for them on a Wednesday until they showed up. But I didn't know how many times it would take her to hit me before I got knocked into Wednesday, so I never gambled on it.

The point is, these people were not fooling.

So I went to my parents. Now, when you're six, you've got three levels of begging. And so I went to them and I started my first level of begging, which is to encourage them and let them know that this is a wonderful thing and how their child would be a happy person if he could have the fifteen cents and the box top from the Kix to send away for this thing. I don't remember what it was. But I had to have it. The guy on the radio said I had to have it, and he was right. I *had* to have it. So I told them: "Mom, Dad, guess what?"

You start out with "guess what" because they're not aware of "what."

"Guess what?" I said again.

And they looked at me and I said so forth and so on and it's a wonderful thing, and then I let them know that it also wasn't expensive and that all you had to do was have the box top and fifteen cents! And my father said: "We don't have it."

So I went to level two and that was whining. If you whine and let them know that everybody in the world has one and you're the only child that doesn't have one, you think maybe they'll give in. So I whined and I said: "Mom, Dad, I don't see how you can just leave me walking around the neighborhood and I'm the only one who doesn't have one. It's just not . . . not . . ."

And then you put in the word *fair*.

"It's not *fair*!"

But they didn't say anything. They kept looking at me like *American Gothic* and they just kept staring at me like that and so I had no choice.

I went to level three, which was the release of mucus.

"Ahhh! Wahhhh!"

And I made a big bubble with my mouth and I wailed: "Wahhh lahhhh! Arrhhhh ehhhh!"

And they just kept looking at me until finally my father said: "Uh, we don't have it."

And I had inside of me demons. Oh, yes. And these demons from time to time would tell me what to do and

what to say, but they never shared in the pain when things went bad. And so I learned not to listen to them. But they had capacity to grow. They could grow inside me until they were too big to ignore. And as I stood there they grew and one of them said:

Tell 'em that they're both in their mid-twenties and you don't understand how people in their mid-twenties, each one with a job, don't have eight cents apiece!

And I knew the demon was right and I wanted to say it so bad but I kept seeing the picture of that dog with the mushed-in face. So I just went: "Aaahhhh!"

At this point I hated those two people. I hated them and I didn't like God for giving them to me! I was a nice person. Why did God give me these people? I decided to show them how much I hated them. The only way I could do it was stomping, and so I started stomping around the table while I was yelling.

They said nothing. Did nothing. They just kept looking at me. Then I decided (actually, it wasn't me, it was the demons). And the demons said: *Go on up the steps! Stomp up the steps!*

And I stomped up those steps. I got to my room and I grabbed that door. See, I wanted to show them how much I hated them, let them know I didn't like them. And to show them how much I couldn't stand them, I swung the door shut with all the might of my six-year-old muscles. *Boom!*

Slammed that door! And I locked it. *Shoomp!* For the first time in my six years of living, I locked them out of my room. I was breathing so fast and so hard because the demons were now huge and they had to have oxygen. I sat on the edge of the bed and I thought: *I hope that they both if, if, if they called me from downstairs,*

"Oh please, come give us some oxygen! Please!"

I would just sit there in this room and tell them, "I don't have it."

Because they didn't have eight cents and I had to go out into the street and where people would say:

"Where is your so and so?"

And I would say: "My parents don't have it."

And they would say: "Ha, ha, ha, ha, ha! You're broke!"

And I would have to take this peer pressure and live like this. A broke person! And I hated them because of that.

Then I heard my father coming up the steps and he tried the knob to the door. Now what happened, what I'm about to describe, this happened in a second. I'm going to slow it down and talk you through it, but I swear it happened in only one second! I saw it all!

My father tried the knob, which I heard. I turned and I looked at the door and my father kicked on the door with his foot!

The bolt held.

It was the molding that gave way.

The entire wall and molding came into my room. It's

true! I saw it! And I remember thinking as I looked in the hole that was left: *Gee whiz, you can see how a house is built.*

Because the doorknob went through the plaster and exploded the wall behind the door. I could see the molding and the pipes and the brick and the plaster and the wood. There was dust all over the place. And a family of mice came out coughing and ran away.

I sat on the edge of the bed—I saw all of this—and my father came and stood over me and I remember thinking: *God he's big!*

The demons made an escape through my last orifice and I began blinking 120 times a second. Psychiatrists will tell you I was trying to make my father disappear. But no matter how fast I blinked, he stayed right there in front of me. And he put his hand ever so gently on my shoulder.

Now, I don't know why I did it but I began to sing.

Jee-sus loves the lit-tle children . . .

Alllll the children of the worlllld . . .

Blaaack and brownnn or whiiite . . .

Plea-se don't hit meee in thisss fight . . .

Jee-sus loves the lit-tle children of the worlllld . . .

And then my father said to me: "Son, I'm going to tell you something and I want you to never forget it."

And then he knocked me out.

I know he did it (even though I couldn't prove it) because I had a knot under my eye. My mother was rubbing butter on it—there was no ice in those days—she was rubbing butter on it and it kept getting bigger and bigger and bigger. I think it was bad butter.

But that's the way it was back then. See today, those of you who are going to have children, you can't treat your children like that. You have to get a psychiatrist for yourself and your spouse. You have to knock on the door and ask if you can come into their room, giving them time to get rid of the marijuana.

Don't Ever Do Your
Brother a Favor

WHEN I WAS ABOUT EIGHT, my life changed.

Prior to eight, I had an idea of what life was about. I lived with my mother and father. Alone. Which was wonderful. But then they had two more children. And at that precise time it was my clear understanding—as clear as anything can be to an eight-year-old—that the children they had belonged to them. Not me. But they kept saying: "You watch them."

This bothered me for three reasons:

1. They were not my children.
2. I didn't know how to spell *responsibility*.
3. I was eight.

At eight, I was supposed to play. All of my energy said to play. There was no puberty, so sex meant nothing. I had to play. What else was there? I didn't think about anything else except playing. In fact, I didn't even really think—at least not words and sentences. All that kept running through my little eight-year-old head was a Brazilian song—one of those melodies that only they can write. And though you don't speak a word of the language, you understand the meaning of the lyrics. They say: Play! La, da, da, de, da, play!

And I just loved to play. That was it. Play. I went to school, watched the clock all day until the bell rang, and then I played. I moved on in age and grade after grade with this theory. After school: Play.

So, one day when my brother Russell was two, my mother told me she had to go to work.

"I want you to watch Russell," my mother said.

"Okay," I said.

What else could I say? When you're eight you just have to do what everybody tells you or you get into all kinds of trouble. Old people yelling in your face making your eyelids blink fast.

The problem was that because Russell was two years old he had to stay in the house, which meant I had to stay in the house. Ergo, I couldn't go out and play. But I had to go out and play, especially that day.

So the minute my mother left, I started trying to figure out how to get Russell to stay put in the house so I could go play. Then I got an idea. Maybe this will work, I thought. It has to because I need to play.

"Russ," I said. "You're going to be a man someday."

He was so proud when I said that. He stood there smiling, tugging on his little short pants, twisting his ankles which were covered by little short stockings sticking out of little high-topped white shoes.

"Yeah," Russell said. "I hope so."

I knew I had him with that man stuff, so I kept up the pressure.

"One of the things about being a man, Russ, is learning how to keep your mouth shut. That's the sign of a man."

Russell's eyes were wide. He wanted to be a man so badly. He clamped his hand over his mouth as if to say: See! I can be a man!

"Do you want to be a man?"

"I want to be a man!" Russell said. "I want to be a man!"

"Okay." I paused a long time, looking at him. "I'm going to test you today."

Russell nodded, straightened his back. He was ready.

I motioned to a chair.

"Russ, I want you to sit in this chair and stay there."

Russ nodded, then climbed into the chair.

"Now, I'm going to pretend that I'm outside," I explained. "You won't see me but I'll be looking through every window to see if you move."

Russell nodded again.

"Except to go to the bathroom," I relented.

Russell nodded yet again. I gently touched his little, small, two-year-old shoulder.

"Can you do that, Russ?" I asked.

Russell pushed himself back into the chair. He wasn't going to move. He wanted to be a man!

"I can do it!" Russell exclaimed.

"Because you want to be a man?"

"Because I want to be man!"

I gave him my most benevolent, big brother face. "I think you can make it, Russ." I smiled.

Russell took a sharp breath, overcome by my confidence in him. Indeed, he seemed to be right where I wanted him. But I couldn't take any chances. I had to be sure.

"You look like a strong little boy," I observed. "You are a strong little boy, aren't you?"

"I am strong!"

"And if Mom says to you: Did I leave the house, what do you say?"

Russell stared at me in silence. He blinked a couple of times, but other than that, there was no response.

"Russ! You're taking too long!"

Russell looked suddenly hurt and confused. I wondered if I had lost him. But he came back with the right answer.

"I'd tell her that you didn't go anywhere."

I smiled. Russ smiled. I nodded. Russ nodded.

"My man, Russ," I said, patting his shoulder.

So I went out and I played. And I had everything covered because I knew exactly what time my mother was due back. Ten minutes before she was supposed to return, I raced home.

Russ was still in the chair.

"You moved twice," I said as I entered.

"How did you know?"

"I saw you."

Russell didn't break. He puffed out his chest, looked me in the eye, and said: "Well, I just went to the bathroom, that's all."

I smiled. "I know it."

Russell peered at me for a moment and then asked: "Am I a man?"

I said: "You're a man."

My mother came home.

And hit me.

"I didn't say anything!" Russell blurted out.

I tried to quiet him: "Shhh!" But my mother stepped between us.

"You went out," she said, pointing her finger at me. "And you played ball. I thought I told you to stay here and watch Russell."

Russell immediately started crying.

"I'm not a man," he sobbed.

My mother asked Russell: "What are you talking about?"

"I'm not a man," Russell became louder. "I didn't tell you anything. I'm not a man."

My mother turned to me: "What is he talking about?"

I tried to be nonchalant.

"Just something we were talking about," I shrugged.

"Wait 'til your father comes home!"

Well, I didn't care. I'd just as soon die right there in the chair. But I couldn't help but wonder how it was that my mother knew I was playing. So I asked her.

"A little bird told me," she said.

I tried to figure out how a bird could possibly care about what I was doing and then go and tell my mother. The next day I went out and I looked up in the air. Sure enough, they were up there flying around ready to squeal. I became paranoid. Anytime I see a bird, even today, they can't fool me. I know their job.

But those are the kind of strange things parents lay on you. Little images like that. A little bird told me.

How I Became a
Marked Man

WHEN I WAS IN THE FIFTH GRADE, I took this test. I didn't know what it was, just a test they give you for no reason. About a month later, our teacher, Mrs. McKinney, walked into the classroom, faced the students, and asked: "Guess who is the brightest person in this school?"

I'm sitting at the desk, waiting for the clock to say I can go play.

"Mr. Cosby," she said, answering her own question. All at once, everybody turned and looked at me. I looked back for a moment, then said to myself: "So what? I mean, I'm happy to be the winner but just let me go play."

I didn't think much about it at the time. Certainly, I had no concept of the pressures that tag—brightest person in school—was going to put on me. But from that point on, I became a marked boy. Word spread that I was the brightest person in the school and the brightest in the neighborhood and the brightest in I don't know what. And all the next day, people started giving me things to do.

"You can do it," they would say.

And then I would do it and then they'd say: "Good. Now do this."

And I would say: "But I finished that one. I want to go play."

"No," they would counter, "you can't play. You have to do this. Because you can do it."

It wasn't long before it began to dawn on me that this was not fair. If I was judged to be the smartest person, how come I had to do all the work? It seemed to me that the smart person should just sit there, because he's so smart, and let the other people catch up to him. Therefore, I reasoned, I should be able to sit in a room by myself until they get as smart as me. But, in fact, it worked the other way around.

Now, in the 1940s, there was no special class. You were in what they called "dumb school." And that's where I wanted to go. Because the dumb school people, they were always having fun. They were going on trips. They were going to places like the planetarium and the airport. They went to France. And the people who were supposed to be smart, we were bent over, sweat rolling down smearing the ink on the work paper. We were writing, doing all kinds of work. And the minute you finished, someone would say: "Okay, now you have that and do this. You can do the work."

I was persistent. I kept saying: "Why am I working this hard? Please give my work to those kids."

But it never changed. When it rained, they painted. And they sang. And they had to be happy all the time I thought.

To Mr. Sapolsky with Love

I GRADUATED FROM ELEMENTARY SCHOOL and I picked a junior high school: Fitzsimons. Twenty-sixth and Cumberland. And I had to ride a trolley car from Tenth and Parrish—the number 23 trolley—to Susquehanna Avenue, then on up to Twenty-sixth Street where I walked about two blocks to Fitzsimons.

Seventh grade. I had a lot of fun in seventh grade. Except the thing called homework. Now I don't know what these people thought they were doing, but *homework*? It didn't make sense. If you work all day, why would you want to work when you come home? I figured it was just that old people wanted to annoy you.

My downfall came in eighth grade the day I walked into geometry class. Now, up to that point, I thought I had studied all the math there was. I got it. I can add, subtract, divide, and do fractions. And I'm wonderful on "If a man . . ." If you say to me: "If a man . . . ," I'm perked up.

"All right! Go ahead. How far did he walk? Where'd he go? What'd he do? How much does he weigh?"

But now I run right into a thing called geometry.

Although I didn't know what it was, I soon found out it was a form of math. But I think I've got it covered. I sat down and in walked a short man. He was about five foot seven and had a profile exactly like Dick Tracy. Wore the same sport coat every day. His name was Benjamin Sapolsky.

Benjamin Sapolsky loved geometry. You could tell it in his spirit—the way he turned to the board and how excited he was to point to a triangle and talk for two hours about the degree of the angles of that triangle. And the sides. He loved the sides of it. He loved the base. And he passed out a book on this triangle. And the rectangle. And you had to memorize these things. I kept saying to myself: "Why?" I kept waiting for Mr. Sapolsky to tell me why. But he was just so enthralled with the angle and the degree of it and the radius and the diameter. Oh, he used to just scream out and he did everything except dance. And then he gave out homework.

"Do the following problems at home," Mr. Sapolsky said as he handed everyone an assignment sheet.

"Why can't we do them here?" I asked. "Home is to play. 'Cause I'm like Brazil."

And I sang that little melody that sounded like play. 'Cause home is to play. And home is home. And I never took the book home.

On top of geometry I'm getting tired of English and I'm trying to figure out when we're no longer going to have to take English. Because it's stupid. They keep teaching English. Well, I already speak English. And so does everybody around me. What are we studying it for? And they grade you on it.

"You got a D in English."

What does that mean? My English was so bad the guy on the trolley didn't understand me? And the thing about English teachers is that they made up things.

"This is the subjective clause of the subjunction and put the clause where it's supposed to be and put your commas in the proper places."

Who cares about all that stuff? I'm not writing to anybody. And I don't know anybody who I have to write letters to. People I know live right in the projects. And if I do need to write them, I'll buy a card. Happy Birthday. And sign my name.

So what is all this English stuff? I can read. I read *Treasure Island*. (Because I had to.) I read all of that. And I know Mark Twain. I read all of that. I can read and I can write. And the newspapers are not that difficult. I'm not old enough to go to war so I go right past all that.

So to me, these two things were just stupid. Old people with nothing better to do than bother young people. To stop them from playing. La, da, da, de, da, de, da.

And so I never did the homework. One day, Mr. Sapolsky called me up after the bell rang.

"You're not turning in your homework," he pointed out.

"Well, sir," I responded, "I told you why."

"Yes, I know. But I don't understand how many more relatives you have left who are going to die."

See, whenever I didn't turn in my homework, I told him that Uncle So and So or Aunt So On and So Forth had passed away.

"It seems all these people are dying when you're supposed to turn in your homework," he noted.

"Well, sir, I don't know, Mr. Sapolsky."

Pete Parham had a dog. His dog ate up his homework. I didn't have a dog because you're not allowed to have dogs in the projects. So I just had relatives who died. And to be perfectly frank, yes, a couple of them died three times. Because I forgot who died. And Mr. Sapolsky didn't accept the story that the family thought the person was dead—and told me so—but he got well and they forgot to tell me. So Mr. Sapolsky insisted I owed him all this homework.

Mr. Sapolsky gave an exam one day. Four problems in fifty-five minutes. I finished one—used up twelve pieces of paper. I just read the question and I started to work. Twelve pieces of paper and I handed the twelve pieces in. About four days later, Mr. Sapolsky handed the exam results back and I had an F. But the word *correct* was written on the front page and a note underneath it said: "See me after class."

The bell rang and I went up to him.

"I want to talk to you about your paper here," Mr. Sapolsky said. "Papers. Your book."

He held up my twelve pages.

"You know I failed you on the exam."

"Yes, sir."

"But you got the answer correct. And I followed your philosophy. You're a genius!"

"Thank you."

"For the year four hundred A.D.," he added. And then he continued. "You know, they're past all this now. They don't do this anymore."

He pointed to the top of a page.

"You could use up just this much of one piece of paper if you would just read the book."

I said: "Mr. Sapolsky, I don't want to read the book. I don't like geometry."

"Look at what you've done!" He almost screamed. "You've gone through twelve sheets of paper to get the answer correct. I followed this. Brilliant! Now, if you just memorized what's in the book you could be even better."

I wasn't falling for that stuff.

"But then you'd give me more work," I told him.

"You see me after school."

"But Mr. Sapolsky, I live all the way in North Philadelphia in the projects and it'll be nighttime when I get home."

"You don't work!"

He was exasperated.

"Mr. Sapolsky, I just want to play. Just want to play."

"Don't you want to be anything?"

"Yes."

"What?"

"I don't know."

"You could be a lawyer," he suggested.

"Yeah," I shrugged. "But that's hard."

So I got a D in geometry. I don't know how. But it wasn't over. These people are relentless, man. The second half of eighth grade there was geometry II. And I got Mr. Sapolsky again. He looked at me as he was passing out the books but he didn't even give me a book.

"You don't need one," he said.

There's a high school in Philadelphia called Central High School, founded in 1836 or something like that. When I went to Central, it was an all-boys school, which they said was for very bright boys. And I wanted to go there. Not because I was going to get a fine education but because they had these book covers that said Central High School on them. And when you ride the trolley, the old people look at you and say: "You're very bright, aren't you?"

I took the test and I passed and I was accepted. My mother and father went crazy. Oh, they started kissing me and everything.

And so I went to Central and they had a thing called trigonometry. I thought: I'll be glad when I get through these *ometry* things, man. Too many *ometries*. And the trigonometry professor was Dr. Strup, a retired professor of math from MIT. Why he retired and then came to teach, I don't know. It's sort of redundant, isn't it?

"Well, Strup, what are you going to do?"

"I'm going to go teach."

Dr. Strup was six foot four. And he had a very high voice, which made him sound funny when he went on and on about trigonometry. And oh, how he loved trigonometry.

Early on, he got sick and they called off the class. Someone came into the room and said: "Dr. Strup is sick. Come back tomorrow. You will get a substitute teacher."

Now, substitute teachers are the best. So I couldn't wait. But in walked . . .

Benjamin Sapolsky!

Why he was subbing, I have no idea. But I'm telling you, this man came all the way from Russia to bother me.

He walked in and I guess the feeling was mutual because when he saw me he jolted. He recovered after a few seconds and made a speech about trigonometry and how he was going to be teaching it until Dr. Strup got well. And he turned and he saw these figures on the blackboard. Cylinders. And oh, my God, he went even crazier about the cylinder than he did about the triangle. He was dancing and drawing and turning to us and saying: "Do you see?"

Well, at Central it seemed that these kids came from outerspace because they did see. They were answering and they were loving it.

"Yes!"

"Fine!"

"Incredible."

I just sat back and watched it all.

Pretty soon, Mr. Sapolsky gave an exam and I did my twelve pages.

"Well," he said when he handed back my answers, "you got it right again."

Then he paused for a moment and smiled and said: "F!"

Central was tough—you had to study—but I didn't. I would come home and I would play. La, da, da, de, da, de, da. And a lot of relatives died. And even though the teachers at Central were very sympathetic, they wanted to see the homework after the funeral. And even after the burial, they still wanted my homework.

Then I talked to the school's psychologist and told her I

wanted to leave and she said: "No. Stay." Which was very strange to me because she was punishing me.

So I transferred to Germantown High School. And I stayed in the tenth grade for another three years. Actually, my father encouraged me to quit when he told me I looked as old as the janitor. So I quit. I was finally at the point of freedom and having a ball. I am out, I have a job. I was in the shipping room, lifting boxes and putting them on a truck. Back then I was making like a dollar-something an hour. I got a check, gave half the money to my mother, kept half for myself. I went out. I don't know where I went, I just went out. And there was nobody in the neighborhood. Just old people and young people. And I couldn't play with either one of them. And I got tired. So I went down and I joined the Navy.

"You've joined the Navy to see the world," the Navy recruiter said as he was signing me in.

"No," I replied, "I'm just trying to get off my block."

There's a thing in the Navy called watch. This is where you stand guard and protect something. Now we're at a Naval base that is protected anyway. By real sailors. With guns. And we even have a ship in the middle of the base. On cement. I don't know, but I guess it's ready to go.

They have a list in the barracks: a watch list. If your name is there, opposite your name it gives a time. And they put Navy time. Zero two-thirty. If there's a zero in front of the number, that means early in the morning. That means after midnight. See, when you get past twelve noon they don't stop at twelve and go back to one. They go thirteen, fourteen, fifteen, all the way around. So, this one day I saw my name—William Henry Cosby, Jr.—and my serial number and it said: zero two-thirty to zero four-thirty. A two-hour watch. I'm on the list.

That night, instead of turning in early, I talked to my friend until eleven or so. Then I went to bed. I don't even think I had fallen asleep—it didn't feel like I had fallen asleep—it just felt like I was asleep. So I was asleep but I don't even remember falling asleep in terms of enjoying it. And then a light went on in my face and shone through my eyelids. So I opened my eyes and there it was: a hand holding the flashlight. And the voice behind the light said:

"Are you Cosby?"

For a second I thought: Tell him no. And then I realized: This is the Navy. They know who I am.

The voice asked: "Are you paralyzed?"

"No, sir."

"Then get up!"

So I sat halfway up.

"All the way!"

And he ruined my whole day with that attitude.

I got dressed. Now it's dark. Zero two-thirty. He takes me out to a place, gives me a wooden rifle, with an old-time bolt action, as close as you can get to a blunderbuss. No bullets. And this greenish belt. Which means I'm on watch. I had no bullets. A belt. And a white hat. This is how I was supposed to fight off the enemy?

So he takes me to a place, which is the place where we hang our clothes to dry. It's the clothesline yard. There are no clothes on the line, nothing on the line. And then he said: "Watch this!"

I thought some kind of show was about to happen. I stood there and said: "Okay. What?"

"Look," he barked. "Stand at attention."

So I did. And I said: "Okay, so where is the show?"

"There is no show," he growled. "Watch this!"

Now I'm not going to do Abbott and Costello with this guy. So I just stood there.

"Now you walk from here," he said, pointing to a spot, "and come back to here and you keep an eye on it."

"On what?"

"The clothesline."

I pointed out to him that it was made out of wire.

"It's made out of wire. Who's going to steal it? And why aren't the people who are watching the base doing their job? I could be sleeping."

"You'll do what you're told, sailor!"

So I stood out there with this white hat on and I got sleepy and I got mad because I'm on watch and there's nothing to watch and I felt stupid. And if somebody did come, I'd say: "Halt! Who goes there? I don't have any bullets! Please don't hurt me!"

So the man came back and I was crying and he got in my face.

"I'm not your mother! And you'll hadda, hadda, hadda, hadda, and you'll do what you're told! Hadda, hadda, hadda, hadda, hadda!"

And I wanted to punch him but I knew he'd put me in the brig.

"Yeah, you can think what you want, but hadda, hadda, hadda, hadda!"

I got off watch and I came back. The lights were still off—you're not allowed to turn any lights on—so I went in the shower and I wrote my mother and I told her what they did to me. And I didn't care about commas and semicolons. My mother knew what I was saying. Yes, sir! She sent a letter to the base commander! And thanked him for what they were doing. And told them to do it some more.

I spent three years, eleven months, three weeks, and three days disliking it. I kept telling myself I shouldn't be there and this was my fault. I made this on my own. So the day I got out, I had planned to take all my Navy stuff and throw it into the bay. And I was in Norfolk, Virginia.

But in the meantime I took the GED exam. So when I left the Navy I went by the Temple University bookstore and I said: "What books do you have to read while you're a freshman?"

I bought every one of them. Even from the School of Dentistry. And I was ready. Fired up. Freshman year, nothing got past me. I studied everything.

At the end of my freshman year I was out on the track. Seventy-five degrees. About 40 percent humidity. A beautiful day. And I was just running up and down the middle of the track. I weighed about 178 pounds. In wonderful physical shape. Doing well in all my exams, turning in homework. And adding extra pages because I felt the professor should know that I was able to do that. And a friend of mine came running over to me and he said to me: "Hey, Cos. You made the Dean's List!"

"Oh, Lord!" I reacted. "No!"

"Hey, what's the matter with you?"

And I whined: "I didn't do anything wrong, man. I'm not watching any clothesline. I'm not doing nothing."

"No! That means you're above three point oh."

I smiled.

"Yeah? Tell the Dean to call me."

Junior year is the year in which you begin your student teaching. See, I'm in Teacher's College and I've chosen Teacher's College because there are millions of mes out there. And I'm going to catch every one of them. I'm going to stop them and tell them my story. And they're going to learn and they will know why they going to learn. All this as a physical education teacher.

As a physical education teacher you had a uniform.

Black pants with the creases in them. Leather sneakers. Way before any leather sneakers, teachers wore black leather sneakers. White shirt. And a black bowtie. Long sleeves. Looked like a referee for a boxing match.

Scottie Moyer (one of my fellow students) and I were so proud. As our student teacher assignment we got a junior high school. That's where you catch them. See. When puberty hits. Catch them when they're horny.

So we go to this junior high school and we go to see the principal who is handing us all kinds of orientation material. Also, the principal is telling everyone what class they have, what room to go to, that sort of thing.

"Scottie Moyer," the principal said, "you have physical education, room so forth and so on." And then the principal turned to me and said: "William Cosby, you have geometry."

Geometry? I looked at the principal in disbelief.

"I don't think you understand. I have a bowtie and a white shirt and I am physical education."

"No," the principal insisted. "We've looked at your transcript and you are very bright. You have geometry. Now go to room three oh something."

So I went to the room, opened the door, and walked in. And he was sitting with his back to me but I knew from his sports coat who it was.

"Mr. Sapolsky?"

"Yes?"

He turned around and he looked at me and he recognized who I was. And his chair started to spin around about a hundred miles an hour. And he turned into butter. And he stood up and he said: "You!"

"Yes, Mr. Sapolsky."

After a moment of shocked silence, I said: "Mr. Sapolsky. I'm a physical education teacher. I'm going to graduate from Temple University Teacher's College and teach physical education. I don't know why they gave me this. Geometry."

"Exactly! You don't know anything about geometry."

"Exactly! Mr. Sapolsky. Let's do something about this."

Oh, my goodness, for the first time, Mr. Sapolsky and I were bonding. We walked down that hallway, man, you could feel the heat. And I was saying: "Go get 'em, Mr. Sapolsky, 'cause they don't know." And Mr. Sapolsky went up to the desk—and the desk hit him about at the eyebrows—and the principal came out.

"John!" Mr. Sapolsky shouted, he called the principal by his first name. "John! This boy! You've given him to me?"

"Yes, we have, Ben."

"Then I want to tell you something. This boy . . ."

Mr. Sapolsky raised his hand and pointed it at me. And I know that was going to say: "doesn't know anything about geometry."

But he didn't say it. And I think the reason he didn't say it was because he would then have to say: "I know, because I taught him."

So Mr. Sapolsky turned back toward the principal and gritted his teeth and said: "Is going to be the best geometry teacher!"

Then he glared at me and ordered me to come with him.

"Follow me!"

"But Mr. Sapolsky!"

"You shut up!"

And as I followed Mr. Sapolsky down the hall he made a prediction.

"You will never get out of Temple alive!"

Praise the Lard

I WAS BORN IN 1937, a child of William and Anna Cosby, who were brought up in Virginia, which is considered the South and the land of the oink. My mother and father ate oink. And they loved oink grease. Lard, is what they ate. And they soaked up grease with a biscuit. And they loved butter too. And they sopped and drank and ate grease. Sausage. Bacon. Ham. The oink. They loved it. Fatback. Salt pork. Oink. And I was born with lard all on my head, in the cracks of my arms and the back of my leg. And I tried to explain to my wife that I am addicted to grease. Praise the lard! I love cake. I love pie. I love potato chips. I love salt. Still, she always wants to know: What did you eat today? What did you eat yesterday?

I do not want yogurt. Plain yogurt. It's healthy. Why don't I like it? Because, it tastes like bad breath. And people who push health food on you are relentless, they're just relentless. They keep coming with nothing. They go to what's called the health-food store and come back with a bag of potato chips. Sun-roasted, unsalted. Here. Eat these. But I'm not interested in just making noise. I can do that with those little poppers. I can do that all day. I want to eat! I want sugar. I don't want substitute nothing! I want the real deal. I love real sugar. White. No brown sugar that's been dropped in the dirt. Like I said, I love cake. But only with real sugar. No substitute nothing. I love ice cream. But the sad truth is that because I'm married and I have this wife who controls me, I have to eat like a common thief and crook in the night. Hiding ice cream under the sofa. Looking like a child: I didn't have anything. I mean, you have to act like a child when a grown woman says: Let me smell your breath.

Every night I eat a small pint of ice cream. A small pint. As opposed to a half gallon, which is what I really want. I'm doing you a favor, I say to her, this is a small pint. But she was still worried. So she made me go and have my blood drawn. The test results came back a couple days later.

My cholesterol was 741.

But it's supposed to be. You eat what I eat, it's supposed to be. The doctor started freaking out: "Oh, my God!"

"It's supposed to be 741, man. I eat cake, pie, ice cream."

"You're going to die."

"Yes," I shrugged. "Isn't everybody?"

Because of my cholesterol, my wife—who's in charge of

me—wanted to put me in a home. See, those of you not married long enough don't understand that after a while your wife reads things. Newspapers. And then she leaves articles in the bathroom for you to read.

Big note: Pertaining to you!

So and so is no good for you. You cut it out. Then three months from now it will flip to be the other side. Now the article says: And it will cure this! And then you can go back on it. But she won't show you that note.

So my cholesterol is 741. So what? It doesn't bother me that it's 741. Every once in a while my left arm will go numb. Okay. But if you shake it, the feeling will come back. And I'm not worried about it. Because look—to be perfectly blunt—if you sit on the toilet long enough your right leg will go bad. So? Is that cholesterol?

The following week I was in Los Angeles and I'm on my way to Las Vegas for two nights and then I was going to fly back East. Home. And the doctor called me.

"I'd like to have your blood drawn and checked again," he said.

"Why? I already told you I don't care about my cholesterol."

"Well, there's something else. I don't know what it is but your hemoglobin is low."

Obviously, I was concerned. He reassured me.

"It may be just the machine or whatever but your hemoglobin is low."

"What is hemoglobin?"

"That's the amount of blood you have in your body."

"Well, what is it?" I wanted to know.

"I'm reading ten oh two."

"What's it supposed to be?"

"Fifteen, fourteen. But don't worry."

"Don't worry?" I erupted. "A third of my blood is gone and you're saying don't worry! What kind of doctor are you, man?"

"The same one who said don't worry on your 741 cholesterol."

I wasn't amused. I told him: "You better wake up and get serious now."

So I fly into Las Vegas. Now this is the point, in reality— for just about all of us—that is the point of denial. And it's silly, one's behavior. It's similar to when you're driving and you get sleepy. And all of a sudden you start to talk yourself into the fact that you could take a little nap—and wake up before you hit something. I mean, many of us have been in that situation. That's when you are dangerous to yourself, man. You're driving and you're going: Okay. Now, the road is straight. All right, there we go. And I'll time it. Yeah, there it is. See, I knew that all the time.

And you wake up with lights flashing and you wonder how you got there with the door in your head.

Well, that says something about you. And that type of denial will be everywhere in your life. Especially when it comes to your health. For example, you feel your body and you find a lump. And you say: Okay, man. I've got a little thing right here and it feels like it's a lump but that's okay.

Why don't you go see a doctor?

Naw, naw, it's okay. It'll go away.

You don't want to have it checked because the doctor may say: Ooo! You've got it! That means that you have it. If you don't go, it means you don't have it. And it's better to just not have it. Like a lot of women I know. It's very simple: Go have your breast checked. But they refuse.

Why don't you get a breast exam?

Ah, no. Thank you.

Why not?

Because I may have it.

And if they don't check?

Then I don't have it.

So what if you wait until it's too late?

Well then I have it.

Nobody wants to have it. And if you don't want to have it, then don't go see anybody.

So I don't know why I'm losing all this blood but I'm not going to go have any blood checked. And I'm not telling any doctor anything. Because if you tell them something, they say: Mmmm, hmmm. And then you might have it. So I'm not telling them anything.

Anyway, I did the two shows in Las Vegas and I was feeling dizzy but I thought it was the flu. Because my wife had the flu and I thought I caught the flu from her. But it works on my mind—the dizziness—and so, about two-thirty in the morning I go to this place, the Las Vegas Medical Center. I jog over to the Las Vegas Medical Center from the Hilton Hotel, two-thirty, quarter to three in the morning. And there's just a skeleton crew but they always have somebody who can look at you and take care of you.

I get there and they, of course, knew me.

"I'd like to have some blood drawn," I said.

"For what?"

"Well, the doctor wants to check my hemoglobin."

So this guy came out. He's a doctor, I guess. Three-thirty in the morning, you don't know what you're getting. They could dress up a guy from valet parking, you know? But at least this guy looks like a doctor. There's a stethoscope in his pocket.

"What seems to be the trouble?"

I'm thinking: That's the same thing an auto mechanic asks you. Anyway, I tell him about my hemoglobin.

"Okay," he said. "We'll draw the blood."

All of a sudden, drawing blood didn't make sense to me.

"Now, look. If my blood is low, why are we drawing blood to see if I'm low on blood? Don't you guys have another test to see if there's blood?"

"Heh, heh, heh, heh."

He drew the blood and he handed the vials to some guy

who got on a burro and rode across the desert to Mt. Sinai or somewhere for them to run it on the machine. Stat!

I'm sitting there and he asks me what the hemoglobin was on the last test. I tell him it was ten point two.

"Have you been bleeding from anywhere?"

"Well, not that I've seen."

"Have you had any stomach pain or anything?"

So now, this guy is asking questions. I ain't telling him nothing, man.

"No. I'm not having any pain."

Which I really hadn't. And then I started thinking if I had or not.

"Have you had any dizziness or anything?"

"No."

Which I had. But I'm not telling him. Because then he's going to say I have it.

"Have you looked at your stools?"

"Of course not!"

Which was a lie. As soon as you hit forty, you look at anything that comes out of your body. You can put a Q-tip in your ear, pull it out, and hold it in front of your face and study it. Then you call your wife: "Ahhhh! Dear? What color are your brains?"

"Just in case I look at my stools," I asked the doctor, "what am I looking for?"

"If you're bleeding in the intestine, it will turn your

stools black. Then you will know that you're bleeding from the intestines."

"And that's the one time that black is not beautiful," I joked.

He fell on the floor laughing.

Tranquillity: Just a Thought
While Listening to a Jackhammer

VARG GOOM!

IN ALL THE YEARS I have been performing in Nevada, I have never said: "I want to go sit by Lake Tahoe and look at the beautiful mountains of Lake Tahoe and hear a guy (or two or three of them) on jet skis aggressively going by, ripping up the water and spilling gasoline into the most beautiful lake in the United States of America."

I never said that. Not once.

I remember one evening, I was sitting by the lake with a friend of mine. My friend had this beautiful girl with him and they were enjoying a nice glass of wine and talking and hugging. And we were all relaxing and watching this fabulous sunset, just watching the sun coming down over the tranquil waters of Lake Tahoe. It was wonderful. All of a sudden . . .

Vroom! Vroom! Vroom! Vroom!

Some guy comes out of nowhere on a five thousand

horsepower jet ski and he's going three hundred miles an hour. My friend was so startled he spilled wine all over this lovely girl and she got mad and left and he never saw her again.

Who could possibly enjoy the loud chatter of pistons shattering the tranquillity of such a peaceful scene? Only the riders. The people who operate these things. They're the only people who seem to enjoy rattling their brains. (If they have any.) People on jet skis. People in motorboats. People driving souped-up cars. People riding big motorcycles. I mean, the small motorcycles make a terrible racket too, sometimes even more than the big ones.

God made tranquillity. God made man. Man made noise. Everything else sings or hums. Unless they're angry. Human beings are the only creatures God created that make loud noises to ruin God's tranquillity. And I hope all the noise people are making doesn't make God angry because He's got the biggest noise of all.

Boats

I LIKE GOING OUT ON BOATS, quiet boats, but I don't like to fish. I would rather have someone buy fish and cook it because going out and catching a fish and trying to pull it in or whatever, I really don't see that. I think those days are over. Still, there are some human beings who will go out with a pole and all of that stuff and stand even in contaminated places.

Before contamination, people would go out to a lake that had fresh, noncontaminated fish. A guy would throw out the line, catch the fish, pull the fish in, and have this wonderful dinner. But today these people are fishing in the Hudson. Now when you catch a fish, it's frightening because with the Hudson you don't know what you're going to come up with. You might pull up a dinosaur fish or something like that.

So anyway, I have some friends and they have some boats

and then I have some friends and they have yachts, two-hundred, three-hundred, five-hundred-foot yachts. But I see some people and they have like forty-five-footers and these things bounce in the water. In fact, I observed the following one time.

While sitting in the south of France, the water was rolling, it wasn't rough, no big winds, it was just rolling. The people pulled up their boat so that all of the people on land could see it. It's a part of showing off a boat. People who own boats have to find someplace where the people are sitting looking at the water and then, what they do, is they steer their boat to the dock. Of course, the people sitting there didn't come to the beach to look at boats. The reason they came down to the water was to relax and look at the water. So when a big boat with a big motor suddenly muscles its way in front of the people, that's rude. It's almost like mooning somebody.

The only great-looking thing of that size—thirty-eight, fifty footer, sixty footer—is a sailboat. You can see sailboats but they don't have a noise with them so they look beautiful, especially when they have a sail up. They just sail back and forth and look wonderful. So, generally, the people who really want to show off are these power boaters. They pull up as far as they can without going aground (or whatever it's called) and then they have to back up, which makes even more noise than going forward. Finally, they drop anchor and completely block the view.

These boats, which are bobbing up and down in front of

your face, these boats have seats. People are sitting in these seats and they begin to serve each other drinks. Now, to watch these fools (and I know they didn't mean to entertain me) but to watch these fools come climbing up and out of wherever they made the drinks and the hors d'oeuvres, well, it's just pure entertainment. You see this guy come from belowdeck and put his foot down and he's carrying stuff to his friends who are sitting there with their backs to us showing us that they have a boat and are having a good time. (And at some point more boats come and these people are maneuvering to get a good spot to show off their boat and they don't seem to realize they are fighting to get into a complex where everybody's house looks the same.)

Now, the ship is bobbing up and down and you see the guy put his leg up in the air and then he steps down on an invisible step that he never sees and then he goes left and then he goes right—and the person sitting there just sits—and he hands the sitting person a drink and then the guy turns around and grabs at what he thinks should be there but is no longer there because the boat is bobbing and moving and these people just look stupid. They look like a bunch of drunks.

So I wondered to myself what it must be like sitting in a rocking boat. It must be like sitting in a rocking chair, bobbing up, down, over, sliding, banking like a billiard ball on an opening break. Because at one point you are sitting there—and the boat is bobbing—and you're up in the air a good six feet and then your end goes down and the other person is now up. It's like being on a seesaw. One minute you're talking to someone and the next minute you're saying: "Where did he go?"

And you're wondering where the person went because when you come back down, the person who used to be there is no longer there. He's fallen over the side.

Later that day, a friend of mine wanted to take me out on his flat-bottom boat, called an LSD, and this was before they made it into a drug. I told the fellow I'd rather wait until the water was smooth but he insisted that the small swells didn't mean anything until you stopped. So we went out and stopped somewhere in the middle of the ocean and then he handed me a drink but I was too sick to drink it. See, the flat-bottom boat LSD causes the same problem as the drug LSD only you can see in color when you take the drug and it goes with loud music.

Anyway, somebody brought out a camera and I suddenly realized that the whole idea of this boating thing was to get a picture of a person bobbing up and down.

A Gift from God

A Gift from God

WHEN I TALK ABOUT MY WIFE, I want everyone to know that it is my general feeling that the relationship I have with my wife—which I speak about and I write about or I write about and I speak about—that it happens I'm pretty sure I'm on about 80, 88 percent. Some people may not understand, some people may feel it is very, very harsh what I'm saying. But I think that after you examine what I have said, you'll find I'm not really saying negative things about my wife as much as I'm talking about myself and my relationship with myself and my wife.

Our relationship is one of love and respect but it is also a relationship of two people who are living together, going on pretty close to forty years of living together. Now you cannot have this kind of long-term relationship without having competition, without someone saying: "Look I told you this three times already! Why are you asking me this again!"

This doesn't mean that the person doesn't like the other person. It just means that you've lived with the person long enough and you feel very comfortable in telling them that they're not too bright and they're not retaining things. So I would like people to read the following sentence and retain it.

All statements made pertaining to my wife are made out of love and with deep respect.

Okay. Now. Having said that, let me tell you that I remember a dinner. I don't remember the name of the gentleman who's sitting next to his wife but he told me they had been married fifty-seven years. And so, I asked him a question.

"Fifty-seven years? Do you love her?"

He put his arm around her and he smiled and very softly he said: "She's a gift from God."

And I feel the same way about my wife and I would like to thank that gentleman for saying that. And he wasn't even a songwriter or a poet, I don't think.

Passenger Abuse

Passenger Abuse

I REMEMBER CLEARLY HOW, when I was fifteen or sixteen years old, my friends and I used to make fun of old people driving. We'd get angry with them—people around fifty—and we laughed at them a lot. As a matter of fact, once we all got our driver's licenses, the one thing we always commented on was the slow-driving old person ahead of us and why couldn't we get these people off the road. And, of course, we let them know they were a hazard to us and then we just zoomed right on past them.

Well, now my friends and I are old people.

I'm sixty-three years old. There are certain times when I feel sort of stiff, and then there are times when I hurt. Even though I have these problems, they don't stop me. My friend Jason, who is sixty-seven years old, has had a quadruple bypass and some other assorted operations. He's been in and out of the hospital quite a bit. Whether they took things

out and put them back I don't know, but there's a certain
percentage of his body that's now been replaced with veal
parts. And whatever. Today, more and more, doctors are putting things into people to keep them alive with all kinds of
electric impulses.

One day, Jason was driving and I was riding with him
and something in his car—like a dinging sound: *ding, ding,
ding*—went off. And knowing what I know about him
medically, I started to hit him in the chest and give him
mouth to mouth because I didn't know what in his body
was going off. I was very happy to find out that it was just
the automobile. But Jason wasn't very happy. With a look of
disgust on his face, as he wiped his mouth, he said: "I don't
care what sounds you hear coming from my body. Unless
I've passed out cold, don't you *ever* put your lips on mine
again!"

Anyway, I swear to you, Jason now drives exactly like
those old people we used to make fun of. I have known this
fellow for fifty years and I will tell you he was one of the
first people to make fun of old people and now he's driving
just like them.

So one day I was in the passenger seat—Jason was driving—and I experienced what I call "passenger abuse."

Now, this man will get into the left-hand lane of any
highway, freeway, anywhere, and he will drive in that left
lane forever. He just gets in the left lane and stays there.

So here he is in the left lane. Here I am, an innocent passenger. Cars are passing us on the right, blinking their lights, beeping their horns. People are driving erratically, pulling out from behind us, pulling up beside us. And here's where the passenger abuse comes from. The people who have to pass us on the right, they're angry. But they make the faces at me. I get faces, I get fingers. There was one woman, she drove alongside us for maybe seven miles, just yelling, yelling, yelling. But my friend just kept looking straight ahead while I took all the abuse.

I tried to be nice to my friend. I didn't want to say anything to hurt his feelings. So I very nicely said to him: "You know, Jason, there's a lot of people passing us on the right."

And, with a very straight face, keeping his eyes on the road, he pointed to his speedometer and he said: "Those people are speeding."

This Will Never Change

CUCKOO WASP

LIMBURGER FLY
LAYING EGGS
ON A GYPSY MOTH LARVA

HOUSE MOSQUITO PUPA

DUNG BEETLE
(MALE)

THINK OF A FRIGHTENING MOMENT that you've had in your life. It could be while driving, flying, swimming, or something like that. And I'm sure that when you think about it, it's still frightening. When you think about it, does that incident provoke:

    a. hair rising on the back of your neck
    b. goose pimples all over your skin
    c. a mental moment of chilling white flashes
    d. shivers for a split second

Good. Now you're frightened. So I will tell you my frightening moment. Actually, this moment has happened several times in my life and each time it was just terrifying.

I have known nothing more frightening than someone I

know and trust telling me that something is crawling on my neck. First of all, these people don't know how to do it. You are standing there innocently, you are not even thinking about anything particular except that you are there. All of a sudden this person who you know and trust turns to you and—with horror on their face—says to you: "Bill, there is something . . ."

And they don't get to "crawling," the word "crawling" doesn't come out of their mouth,

"Bill there is something cra . . ."

And then they take their hand and they start to swing at you.

Well, first of all, when I see their face, filled with horror, and they say: "Bill there is something cra . . ."

Well, I immediately react. My shoulders go up, my face, it gets a horrible look. I'm frightened. My neck draws in. I don't know what it is that's crawling, but there is something crawling on me. And I don't know where to look. I'm trying to look and then this person starts to swing away at me and they never get it. They *never* get it.

"Where did it go?" they say. "What happened to it?"

And now you're wondering: What is it? Is it going down my back? And you ask the person what was it and they can never say.

"It was a sparrow. No, it was a bat. No, it was a spider. No, it was a small ant. No, it was a ladybug."

And on and on.

It appears to me that this is the most frightening thing that can ever happen, having someone tell me that there is something crawling on me because they just don't know how to do it and then they start slapping at you and they never kill the damn thing. They lose control, they panic, they start yelling—I mean, you can't see the thing—so they panic and they're loud.

"Oh, my God!" They yell.

You look at them and wait for more information.

"It's on your . . ."

But before they even finish the sentence they start slapping you and hitting you and jumping back off of you and you still have no idea what it is. And so it's left up to you to figure out what in hell this thing is. I mean, how big is it? How dangerous is it? Will it kill you? And it's all the most frightening thing I have ever had happen to me in my life.

My friends do it to me.

"Oh, my God! You have something . . ."

Slap! Swat! Slap!

My wife does it to me.

"Billy. You have something on your neck."

And then she comes with the hand raised and I stand there and I don't know what it is. I almost want to start crying. Sometimes I revert to a reaction I had when I was a little kid and used to get all excited when someone said to me: "You know, your finger's bleeding."

And I'd scream: "Ahhhhhh!"

That's what it feels like when someone tells you that you have something crawling on your neck. To me that's the most frightening thing.

Ingrown Hair

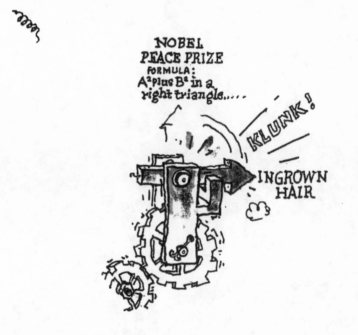

THIS IS REALLY A MALE, MALE THING and I don't know where it ranks in terms of sheer frustration but it's pretty high. It has to do with, on the face, an ingrown hair in the beard area. Now this thing is under the skin and it is forming a lump of some sort and when you touch it, it hurts—it lets you know in no uncertain terms that it is there. And then you shave and keep looking and you can't see it, but you know the lump is there. I had one such lump many times and each time I became angry with it because it wouldn't come out. I would pinch it and liquid would come out. (I don't mean to make anyone sick: just a small amount of liquid would come out.) But the lump wouldn't come out and it would still hurt.

So I would begin to squeeze it and pinch it from time to time and it would be this annoying little appendage that wouldn't come out, a visitor in my face that I did not want.

And there have been times—even during great dinner conversations with very important people—that I thought constantly about this thing because I would put my thumb or my finger to my face and I would feel it and it was there, this persistent little lump. I could be listening to a great scientist describing some formula for which he or she has received a Nobel Prize and in the middle of this interesting conversation, which is being told only to me, my mind would switch to this hair that is in my face. And me and this hair would have some tender moments—it was so tender to the touch—and I would be preoccupied with this hair because it wasn't coming out. And all of this can become very, very competitive no matter how brilliant the conversation.

Last week, I got one of these lumps. I was sitting, writing, and all of a sudden I remembered it and I put my finger to my face and it was there. I rubbed it with my thumb and abandoned whatever I was doing. I went upstairs to the bathroom, got out the alcohol, and I declared war on this thing. I punctured myself with a sterilized sewing needle and I dug in looking for this ingrown hair, this hair we all know, every man knows, by the time he reaches forty. By then, you know what this thing is. You know that this is that hair.

Now, my skin is very, very dark brown. Therefore, I am able to pick up a gray hair as well as a black one. I don't know what people with lighter skin coloring do when their hair turns gray and gets closer and closer to their skin color, whether or not they can see this hair. Anyway, it requires time to defeat this thing and, in most homes, the bathroom is really not a place that is comfortable for picking your face. But you go there because, if you are a male, the bathroom has everything to do with shaving and after all, this is a hair.

You don't sit down to shave your face, but in order to get this hair—which is now becoming Moby Dick—you sit down. It is now you and Moby Dick and you become so angry you want to tear off your face. You want to reach up and grab that spot and just rip it out—you don't care what you have to do—and as time goes by you become a mad person, a madman. Not angry. Mad. Let's say, you've made seven attempts at getting this hair. It hurts when you shave, you feel it. When you touch your face it says "Hello" because it is very tender and it hurts, but you can't get it. You don't know where it is. It is hiding under the skin and, in your madness, you decide to wage a full-scale attack on this lump. You'll do anything, even ram your face full speed ahead, just to get that hair.

So you get a sewing needle, alcohol, tweezers—that's all you really need besides some tissue paper and a great mirror—and you imagine yourself an expert surgeon. Mind you, the older you get the more you're going to have to get out the other glasses too because if you just have your reading glasses, they are not going to help to magnify the mirror. Obviously, two magnifying glasses do not make a stronger picture. So you have to hope that the magnifying mirror gives you a great picture of the field, the field being where you know that hair to be. Once you map out the field, your finger will tell you, either the thumb or the index finger, will tell you exactly where this hair is hiding.

So now you're ready. You know one thing right now: you hate this hair. So you wipe your skin with the alcohol to clean the area, wash your hands, and use alcohol on your fingertips because there is going to be plenty of pinching and squeezing going on. You pull your skin and you look and there is the lump, but it's now in a larger area and when you squeeze it fluid comes out. (I will not describe the fluid because you may be reading this book while you are eating, but you know the fluid that I am talking about.)

God only knows how much skin you have if you stretch it out to whatever, but it really has come down to this small area on your body and you couldn't care less if you are going to damage your skin. You don't care if you do nerve damage. You don't even care if you scar your face. All you know is that you have to get this annoying displaced hair.

Maybe it's been a good four months that this hair has been your constant companion. Yes, my friends, it is possible that an ingrown hair can be under your skin for that long. The important thing now is not to forget that you've made many attempts with these same materials and utensils: a sewing needle, alcohol, tissue paper, and tweezers. But this time, you're going to get that hair!

Now doctors, dermatologists, will say things like "follicles" or whatever, I don't know any of that mess, I'm just telling you what I'm looking at in the mirror. You go in until you find a hole where a hair could come out. This is a basic, entry-level lesson to learn because if you just go in on skin, you just go in punching skin, you're going to scar your face, which at this point you're a madman and you really don't care. You're going to scar your face if you go in where there's no hole already. Find the hole where at least you know a hair could come out or should have come out but hasn't yet.

One thing that I found to be very interesting is that while you're digging away with the sewing needle—gouging, punching, poking, and making yourself bleed—you salivate. I don't know exactly why. Psychiatrists would probably find it quite fascinating to study this phenomenon. While you are stabbing and giving pain to yourself, you are salivating and you are sucking air in to keep the saliva from dripping down the side of your face.

Well, I must tell you that after about seven months, I finally had success. I went into the right hole and then I dug up to the surface hoping to capture it on the tip of the needle and pull it out through the hole. There was a little blood, just a little blood, because I was digging and probing, but when I took the alcohol and the tissue paper and I wiped off the blood, lo and behold, I looked and there it was!

It wasn't a Great White, it was a Great Black hair. When it first came out it was short, short enough that if I wasn't very careful, I could have lost it. I also wasn't sure if it was, in fact, coming out of the hole I had gone into. What if I had dug in and interrupted a hair that wasn't an ingrown hair?

Slowly, I wiped again, stroking down with the tissue paper and alcohol. When I took the tissue away, the hair was longer! So I took the tweezers and I had hope. See, this is another part of the whole experience—hope. You are hoping for something, you're hoping that this is it, this is the hair. You're thinking about it and suddenly you become angry again. You become so very angry with this thing that has been in you for months invading your face, not behaving, itching, hurting, making you think about it, hiding from you, moving away like Moby Dick.

So I grabbed the tweezers in order to really enjoy this coming out. And I clamped onto the hair with the tweezers and I pulled. And pulled. And pulled. The length—when I finally stopped pulling—had to be an inch and a half and it was doubled around!

At last! I had conquered the Great Black! But then, on the side of this black hair, was a Great White at least three inches long! My, God! The Great Black and the Great White were partners! It was like an episode of *I Spy* in my face!

I rested for a moment because I couldn't believe what I

was seeing. And I knew I was getting near the end—I could feel it. I could feel all that was underneath the tissue was giving some resistance so I was careful not to let go. And I thought about what the dermatologist said to me once: "When you do these things, don't pull them out, cut them."

Well, I have a problem with that because I've got it now and I want to pull so I can be sure to get it all. But how do I do that? See, I can't really capture it and pull it all the way out. Pulling it all the way out endangers the whole operation. And if you lose what you've gained so far, it can go ingrown again. That's why they ask you to cut it once you've got it out of the hole. But I hate these two hairs and I want to pull them out and I want them out for good. And there they both are, just hanging out of my face, longer than anything I've ever had on my face, and I wiped with the alcohol and tissue paper and I just stood there for a moment and then I pulled. Slowly, I looked. I had the Great Black. But the Great White had snapped back in the hole.

Why Dave Schembri's Friend Is Still Alive

THERE'S A FRIEND OF MINE—Dave Schembri—who's been missing for some time because he's been in recovery from divorce. But now he's back on the scene and he managed to find his old buddies who he had to get rid of when he got married.

So Dave goes back to the old neighborhood, to his old buddies who are all married now, and for some reason the wives of his old buddies are willing to accept him. Now Dave's about forty-three, forty-four years old, so maybe it's his age that doesn't bother the wives. Maybe wives can just look at a person and tell whether or not they're stable, that this is a person who, in fact, is not a person who's going to bring into their homes that which is not accepted.

So, one day Dave was with his buddies and I met him at a vineyard near where I was performing. They had bought tickets for my show and asked if they could come backstage and say hello. I said fine. No problem.

After the show, they came backstage. Dave was dateless but there were six guys who he had grown up with and they had all brought their wives. After a round of introductions, out came the cameras and we were taking pictures and all the wives and everybody were happy and cheerful. There was one fellow who was with his wife—who I found out was his second wife—and Dave said that this guy was an amazing example of survival. I said: "What do you mean?"

"Well, Bill, he was in surgery for the zipper!"

And Dave said the guy had a, let's say, a sixteen-uple bypass. (To me, sixteen times is no longer a bypass, it's: "We're going in!") Anyway, they did a SWAT on this guy and he died three times.

"Man," I said, impressed. "Three times?"

I looked at him and he was smiling. He was a strong-looking guy, very strong, overweight, but strong-looking. I guessed he was probably forty-six years old, something like that, and I asked him: "Is it true that when you die that there's this light?"

"Yeah," he answered.

"Wow," I said, "you saw the light three times!"

"Yeah."

"But each time you came back."

"Yeah," he said, then added for emphasis: "Oh, yeah!"

I was curious.

"Why did you come back?"

"All three times I saw my ex-wife," he said.

Which I figured absolutely wasn't possible.

"You saw your ex-wife? Really?"

"Yeah."

"And what did she die of?" I wondered.

And he said: "That's why I kept coming back! She ain't dead yet! I just kept seeing her in that tunnel with her fist balled up—my ex-wife—and I kept saying, She ain't dead, she ain't dead, she ain't dead. I don't know where I'm going, but I've got to come back to life, I've got to come back!"

Grandparents

GRANDFATHERS AND GRANDMOTHERS ARE PURE PEOPLE. I was at Central High School when my paternal grandfather, Samuel Russell Cosby, took me aside and said: "You shouldn't play football. I know you want to play football but you shouldn't play football."

"Why not?" I asked.

"Because you're fifteen years old. Fifteen-year-old boys' bones are brittle."

Now, my grandfather worked in a steel mill and his job was to hold the steel while this huge hammer came down and pounded this white-hot steel into some sort of form or shape. That's all he did for a living. He'd just pick up this white-hot piece of steel with these salad forks, huge salad forks, and put the steel under the hammer and turn it the right way. If you don't turn it in time and the hammer's coming down, you're going to get a vibration at the end of the pole you're holding. But I never really questioned whether Granddad was a doctor or not. It's just that Granddad was telling me that my bones were brittle and that I shouldn't play football.

"You shouldn't play football until you're around twenty-three, twenty-four years old."

Well man, I'm fourteen, and I'm going to be fifteen, so to be twenty-four, I'm almost dead. I mean, there's no life. You're past college, where are you going to play football after that? So Granddad essentially was telling me not to play football at all. But football was my love and I had these aspirations, these dreams of touchdown, touchdown, touchdown!

Anyway I thanked Granddad—which is what I usually did whenever he gave me information that I didn't want to pay attention to—and he gave me a quarter for listening to him and then he gave me information on what to do with the quarter.

You see, in 1944, my Grandfather started giving me quarters to listen to him. Each time he gave me a quarter, he said: "Take the quarter and put it in the bank."

Then he started telling me about the interest on the quarter and how at the end of twenty years it would be a lot more. He kept coming up with these numbers that were so far away from any concept I had in my life. I kept thinking, I'll be an old person by then. Now is when I want to enjoy this quarter. I don't want to enjoy this quarter when I'm old after twenty years of 3½ percent interest on twenty-five cents. Who knows what I will like in twenty years? I may not like ice cream anymore in twenty years. I may not like candy bars. I mean, there may not be any candy bars in twenty years. So I have to eat this stuff now. I have to. Soda, I have to have that now.

So, sure enough, I'm at Central High School and I saw a notice on a bulletin board: Junior varsity practice. But first of all, you must weigh 155 pounds. I said: Well, I've got that covered. At five feet, ten inches tall and weighing 135 pounds. But nobody can really tell. And when I went to sign up for junior varsity, there was no stepping on a scale. So I just told them I weighed 155 pounds. (Thank God I only weighed 135 pounds or else they'd have made me a lineman.)

So I went out for the football team and I made it in. The coach knew quite a few of the boys—he had his favorites— but somehow I was a great practice player so I made the team because the coach thought I was a good practice player. I worked hard and so by the time the first game came—against Simon Gratz—I was starting left halfback for Central High School.

I don't know what play it was, or what quarter, but I got a pitch-out and as I was rounding left end, the kid in front of me missed the block on the left end and I jumped up into the air and the kid stood up and I went down head first. You know, mathematically you have to make certain decisions and then, of course, emotionally you have to make certain quick decisions in life. In this particular case I had to make a choice. Do I let my head hit? Or my shoulder. Which is more valuable, my head or my shoulder?

I moved my head out of the way.

But I couldn't clear my shoulder. I landed on my shoulder. It didn't hurt, really. I mean, there was a hollow pain, I guess, and it was all over my shoulder, but it didn't really hurt. However, I found myself not able to push up with my left arm, whereupon all of the fellows started to laugh at me. (This was a side of human behavior I wasn't really quite ready for.)

A man that they called the school doctor came out on the field. It was cold, so he had on a topcoat. This man examined me out in the cold—there was no locker room—and it's cold. Cold! Now, I can't move my arm so he says wiggle your fingers or do something. And he asked me to take off my shirt. Anyway, I don't know how, but with great pain every now and then, this jersey came off and he put a sling on my arm. And this man that the public school system called a doctor said I had a bruised muscle. He didn't say go to the hospital, get X-rays, he just said you have a bruised muscle. So I went home and my mother took one look at me and asked me what was wrong with my arm. I told her I had a bruised muscle. My mother said: "That thing is broken."

"No, Ma. The doctor said it's a bruised muscle."

"You take off your shirt," my mother said.

And I had the worst time getting my shirt off. Every time I moved my shoulder it was like somebody took an ice pick and just dug into it and I was in the worst pain. I'd played football and so I was used to pain, but nothing like this. And so she put an undershirt on me. I never had pajamas. I didn't start wearing pajamas until I got rich, I guess.

Even in the Navy you don't have pajamas—you wear your underwear to bed and you get up and you change it. So I didn't start wearing pajamas until much later. My first pair of pajamas were from Brooks Brothers and they don't make them anymore. I don't even remember what they looked like. I just remember going back and trying to get some about ten years ago and they said they didn't make them anymore.

Anyway, I'm there in my T-shirt and my underwear and my mother went and got some Watkins liniment. In those days there was a "Watkins Man." I don't know what people do today, but in those days whatever you sold, whatever company you worked for, you didn't really have a name, you were the so and so man. The Fuller Brush Man. The Avon Lady. And so he was the Watkins Man.

And then there was the Bread Man. We preferred Freihoffer over Bond. You know, people get brand names, even if—see, we weren't poor, we were broke—but even broke people have brand names that are their favorites. You don't know why, but it's just the brand you like. For instance, there was a syrup called Allega, Allega syrup. If you're from the South, Georgia, say, you know about it. I was born in Philadelphia, but my parents were from Virginia. So we had Log Cabin. Log Cabin was our maple syrup.

I went to a guy's house one day and they had a pancake leftover and they said would you like this pancake. I said yes and they put Almost Butter on it. This stuff was in a plastic bag and you burst this red bubble that was in this bag and you kept squishing it until it turned the color of butter. I don't know what it tasted like white, but I would imagine you get the same thing only without the number two red dye.

And so then I put on this Allega syrup, which took a half hour to come out. It just kept coming, just kept coming. Finally, it hit. It was so slow when it hit the pancake, it made a sound. And then I cut it, I guess, but I didn't care for the flavor. See, it's all relative to your taste.

The Watkins Man, he sells Watkins products and in those days I remember Watkins liniment, which was good for whatever muscle problems you had. It had a linimenty, kind of an alcohol smell to it. We also had Watkins cough medicine, which I liked very much, not for myself, but just for giving to my brother Russell. Three or four tablespoons and he would sleep through World War IV and V.

So my mother put the Watkins liniment on me and put a towel on me and I laid there. Suddenly, the door opened.

It was Granddad.

At the time we lived in the Richard Allen project in North Philadelphia at Tenth and Parrish. Granddad lived in Germantown. And for Granddad to get to our house, our apartment in the projects, he would have to take the number 23 trolley to Tenth and Parrish, but he would have to get to the trolley by way of bus. I don't know how, but I think it must have been a good two and a half mile ride or whatever, which Granddad didn't do. Everybody said that. They'd say to me: "You know Granddad doesn't ride. Granddad walks to work every day and then walks home."

Granddad had a Victory Garden. The Victory Garden, of course, was because of the war. You got seeds and if you had a small piece of land with dirt, you grew your own tomatoes, cucumbers, and other easy things like collard greens or kale, whatever bugs and spraying from high places couldn't destroy. So Granddad had his own Victory Garden. He'd walk to work, then he'd come on home and tend to his garden, so that was five miles.

But Granddad rode the trolley car that night because it was after work. He walks in and I'm on the sofa.

"How do you feel?" he asked.

"All right."

Granddad rubbed my shoulder.

My father came home and saw everybody looking at me.

"I want you to carry on," my father said.

That's what he kept saying, over and over.

"No matter what happens, I want you to carry on. You're the firstborn and I want you to carry on."

He told me all of the things that he could have been but wasn't and he said it was up to me to carry on. To be a pro football player was one of my assignments to carry on.

Well, when my father saw me there with this towel on my shoulder, he kind of looked at me like a prize cabbage that was eaten by worms and he couldn't show it at the fair anymore. Dreams hurt when they die.

So he turned to his father, my grandfather.

"What happened?"

"Junior's playing ball," Granddad said.

"His arm is broken," my mother chimed in.

"No, Ma," I protested. "He said it was a bruised muscle."

"But you can't move it without jumping to the ceiling," she said. "That thing is broken!"

"Well, whatever happens," Granddad said, "let me know if you need anything."

And Granddad gave me a kiss and he rubbed my hand.

"I heard about what happened to you," Granddad continued, "so I just wanted to come down and make sure you're all right."

"Thank you Granddad."

He never said anything about telling me not to play football. He said whatever you need, just let me know and I will be here.

My mother and father asked him if he wanted dinner or anything and he said no and he went back to the kitchen with them. I sent both ears back there to listen to what he was saying. But I still couldn't hear.

Then Granddad walked back to me, kissed me good-bye, and gave me a quarter. But he didn't talk about the bank.

I couldn't sleep that night. There was no position I could get myself into that, when I moved, the ice pick didn't go in that same spot. My mother and father got up, and remember—these are people who are broke—so we had to go to the Einstein Medical Center, the Einstein Medical Center Emergency Ward. We go in and they sent us to the clinic. (Clinic, for those of you who have never looked this up, is a French word which means "sit there until you heal.")

So, my mother is sitting on my left and my father is sitting on my right and they're looking like American Gothic without a pitchfork. I'm the pitchfork.

There was a man sitting not far from us—and I will never forget this—holding two thumbs in his right hand. There's no thumb on his left hand. And some doctors, well there were, I don't know, it's like a gaggle or what, a gaggle of geese, or whatever, a herd of buffalo, a pack of rats. What are seven doctors walking past a man in the clinic who has no thumb on his left hand? A "what" of doctors? A posse? No. A posse is going after something, so you can't say that.

So there's a gaggle of doctors and they're talking in Latin terms and mumbling things. And then they hit these double doors and they disappear. And you sit there and if you weren't sick, it would be an entertaining moment because it's always double doors.

And then the double doors open and there's this woman, Florence Nightingale. She looks around but she doesn't call out a patient's name. She just stands there and looks and then goes back in. It's like: Hey! Do something. Say cuckoo, cuckoo, cuckoo, and then go back in.

Now from the left side comes another gaggle or pack or envelope of nine doctors and there's an old one leading them and they're all saying: "So the hyperextended . . . mumble, mumble, mumble."

And they walk past the poor man with the two thumbs on his right hand. Then they walk past a woman who's delivering her own baby and they don't even look at her, they just keep on going. Now comes a black man who has a hatchet in the top of his head and he sits down and the doctors go by and nobody pays any attention to him. They keep on walking. Then the nurse comes out without saying cuckoo, cuckoo.

I don't remember how it happened, but I think my father stood up—he's five eleven and all these doctors were about five six or five seven—and I don't remember him cursing, I just remember him saying: "My son is sick and you are going to take care of him, aren't you?"

So this old doctor said: "Yes, we are."

My father and I went in. My mother stayed outside to fill in the papers because she's the only one who knows about everybody in the family. Most mothers know about everybody. Mothers fill out papers. Even if you're the CEO of a company, your mother will fill out your medical papers for you because your mother knows everybody's blood type, she knows everybody's address, she knows every ailment.

Here's what mothers know.

Mothers know how old your siblings are. You never know how old your siblings are. Mothers also know how old your father is. And mothers know what you've had. You don't know what you've had. When you fill out the insurance papers yourself, and it asks "did you ever have this," you just say no, no, no, no. So that's why mothers have to go to the clinic with you because they know how to fill out all the blanks.

So they've taken X-rays and the old doctor is showing them to me and my father and discussing them with these young doctors. From what I could understand, the head of the humerus had snapped, and that's not very humorous. They put a cast on me that was called a hanging cast. The elbow joint is in a 90-degree angle and the cast weighs about sixteen pounds. The weight of this cast, this heavy cast, is going to pull the humerus down where the head will

shift into place and it will become one again with the rest of
my bones.

I guess it didn't work too well because I became the
only person who can enjoy swimming in small pools. You
see, due to the malfunction of my left shoulder, I can only
swim in a small circle, and that's the backstroke as well as the
Australian circle. I don't have a crawl, I have an Australian
circle and I have a back circle.

So I went home with the cast and I stayed out of school
eight weeks. Granddad came to see me again, kissed me on
the forehead, and rubbed my arm. And he gave me a quarter. But he never said I told you so. He just handed me the
quarter and said: "Get yourself some ice cream. It's got cal-
cium in it."

When you graduate from college, yes, you do have a degree,
and yes, you have been studying the great writers with great
professors and lecturers. You've figured out some answers to
some pretty difficult questions and you've written some
pretty good papers yourself. But you shouldn't think that
college can give you anything more than an education. It
cannot teach you how to think. And you should never feel
that, because you have an education, you are brighter than a
person with a lesser one.

One day in debate class—I was at Temple University—

the professor asked the students to come up with a position on a certain question and then defend that position. The question was: Is the glass half full or half empty?

Now, this question seemed unanswerable. All my studying, all the books I read, all the education I had received couldn't help me. My way of approaching the problem was to say the glass was both half full and half empty. But the professor had told us to take a position one way or the other and be prepared to debate it. I thought about it the rest of the day but nothing came to me.

So I went home that night—and my grandmother was there—and she saw me concentrating and so she asked me what was the matter.

"I'm supposed to figure out if the glass is half full or half empty," I told her.

Without a moment's hesitation, in a split second, my grandmother shrugged and said: "It depends on if you're drinking or pouring."

How You Can Chip Your Teeth and Pull a Ligament

I WOULD LIKE TO SAY SOMETHING about plastic packaging and the sealing thereof. I realize that these things are sealed because people steal. I don't like people who steal, never have, even when they took things from me, even when they didn't take things from me. I never liked people who steal. But, surely if you want somebody to make something that is childproof, you go get people who seal things in plastic to keep people from stealing in stores.

I am holding something in my hand, something that I purchased. This is mine, but it is sealed in this plastic. The instructions written on this plastic are telling me everything about this thing that I purchased except how to get the product out of this damned plastic. There is also stuff in French, but even in the French that I can make out, it doesn't say where to go to start to open this plastic package.

I am working my thumb around and I am popping the

edges, hoping—as I would with most normal things—that if you take one thumb, place it on one side, and then take the other thumb and place it on the other side, and then pull away, gently, that there is one side that gives way. But this plastic container does not give way. Any way. And it is also eyeteeth proof. I tried to bite down with the incisors, the sharpest teeth known to meat-eating animals, but this plastic rejected my teeth. I could not bite through it.

But wait! I found an opening. Right here. There is a lip. I'm now pulling on this lip, only to find that the lip is the only thing to come apart—not the container. And it comes apart just enough so that I suddenly find my thumb stuck inside the package. And I am bleeding because obviously I wasn't supposed to go in this way.

Now I'm telling you, I'm doing this as gently as I can, but I am bleeding very badly—the thumbs, both thumbs—and I am thinking that those people who had made the plastic sealing deliberately put little razor blades in here so that whoever's trying to steal this is sure to cut himself or herself.

But what about people who buy it? They shouldn't be getting cut. As I said, I don't like people who steal. But there has to be a better way to keep people from stealing while, at the same time, letting the people who buy stuff be able to get to it.

Right?

Seating Arrangements

IN THE BEGINNING OF SOCIALIZING, when you're young, teen-agers, you go to a restaurant, and you pile in because nobody really belongs to anybody and those who do, if somebody belongs to somebody—boyfriend, girlfriend, whatever—then they just slide in and that's it. See, so and so sits next to so and so who's his girlfriend or maybe a guy sits across from somebody he likes. Whatever. It just all works out somehow. Then, when you get into your late twenties, thirties, people start to get married and you socialize, oh, maybe in the home, someone's apartment. A dinner, birth-day party, whatever the celebration is.

Okay. Dinner's ready, everybody come on, let's sit down. Okay. John, what we want to do is, we want boy, girl, boy, girl, boy, girl.

Well, I've always hated boy, girl, boy, girl. I like the men at one end of the table, the women at the other.

Now, I don't mind if you begin to howl in anger, just hear me out. The reason is, being the boy all my life, and on my right is a girl and on my left is a girl, I notice that the women lean forward and talk to each other over my food while I lean back on the last two legs of the chair and turn to my right or my left and talk to a man—we talk about sports or something or whatever.

That's all I'm saying.

So if you put the men on one end, everybody can have their conversations and the wives can all start yelling and doing victory laps around the men. Oh yes, it's all very playful, you can see that. The relationship of marriage is such that the women are joking about the men and saying terrible things and men are saying terrible things about the wives.

I remember a wonderful dinner. I don't remember what the seating was, probably boy, girl, boy, girl. I know it wasn't men at one end. Anyway, a friend of mine—as a matter of fact his name is David Dinkins—was celebrating his forty-sixth wedding anniversary with his wife, Joyce. He stood up, and after all the women had toasted Joyce, David commented that Joyce had had to put up with him all these years. The wives all agreed. It was just sort of shameful. We listened to how the women felt Joyce was so wonderful, in fact, their hero, but I noticed that none of the women went into their pockets to chip in for this damned dinner.

(Okay, that's a male chauvinistic statement. I accept it and I will say it again in a court of law.)

So David raised his glass to toast his wife and he said: "For many, many years, Joyce has always said to me: David, if I die before you, will you get married again? And I've always said to Joyce: Joyce, I would answer your question, but I have a problem with the word 'if.' Now, Joyce, once you make a commitment, then I think I can answer that for you."

I too have been asked by my wife if I would marry again if she died first. And I would say to all the young men who think of themselves as rather macho, the answer is obvious. However, a wife is a person who is not looking for that answer. Even though she knows that when you die, if you die first, she'll think about it and then she's going to get somebody else. She's got to. As a matter of fact, I think it's already in her papers. We didn't have a prenuptial but I know there was something written where she asked me to sign and I said: "What is it?"

And she said: "Oh, just shut up and sign it."

And she went away after I signed it.

So when your wife asks you "If I die before you, will you get married again?"—you think she wants a truthful answer from you. I mean, before you can even answer the question she's telling you how your life would be miserable and you would be lonely and that she understands that you would be lonely and you should have someone to talk to, to comfort you after she's gone. But keep in mind, young fellows, this is the same woman who said, not long ago, prior to all this, that if you ever got married after she died, she would come back and haunt you and the woman you were with to the point that both of you would lose all of your hair and you would run out into the street naked and be run over by steamrollers and she would be in the house just laughing, ha, ha, ha.

So anyway, the answer to that question is: No.

Stay on no. Because if you ever get to the point where you want to speak honestly and say, well, I might. Sure, I'd miss you but, truthfully, yeah, I'd probably get married again. If you say that, then that's the night that you're going to . . . how can I put this? Okay. Let me put it to you this way. Wives have the ability to make it snow under the covers. Oh yes, I remember one time, well it's not like it was the one time that I made a mistake, I've made many mistakes, but this particular time she said she was going up to bed. In wife's terms, that means: Get up and let's go. It sounds like you have a choice.

You have no choice.

This is something that is very, very important to recognize and I advise you to pay attention to your father. You notice that this is a man who is not really the idea of what you think a man is, and he isn't. He's not a man. He's a husband. And he's a father. And over the years he has learned—if he's smart—to keep his mouth shut, to go when told, and to stop doing whatever he's doing and to just go do what he's asked to do. This is a smart man and he will live a long time.

So, you see, it is important for you to never say that you will get married again. That's that.

Now let me get on back to David Dinkins. To reiterate. David said: "So Joyce asked me. She said, David, if I die before you will you get married again? I've always said to Joyce: Joyce, I would answer your question, but I have a problem with the word 'if.' Now, Joyce, once you make a commitment, then I think I can answer that for you."

That was David's attempt at humor. But after the laughter died down, David answered the question like this: "And I said to her: Joyce, why would a man, after escaping prison turn around and dig his way back into the prison and go back into the cell again?"

And this I find to be a wonderful answer. There's an old joke that goes around, been around for a long time, that poses the question: Why do husbands die before the wives? And the horrible punch line is: Because they want to. I don't agree with that. I love my wife and to get out of marriage I would not die before my wife. But I will tell you this, I do want to die before my wife and the reason is this: if it is true that when you die your soul goes up to judgment, I don't want my wife up there ahead of me to tell them things.

Now, let me get back to this table setting. At the table
there was David Dinkins and his wife, Joyce, me, who is
sixty-three, and Camille, who is in her late fifties. Now, seating at a table becomes complicated as people get older
because you have to be careful to not put somebody next to
someone because someone said something about a person
and that person heard about it and that person doesn't like
that person anymore. Or maybe this person's company
wouldn't release something for the company that the other
person owns. Or this person doesn't like that person politi-
cally. Or so and so's wife is something and so and so's wife
is something else—you know all that social stuff.

And then there is also a point in time where, as your
friends get into their seventies and eighties, the seating
arrangement then depends on the health of the person. In
other words, it's no longer boy, girl, boy, girl. It is now:
Look, Eddie cannot hear on his left side so don't put him
next to Janice because if you put Janice on his left side, Janice's dentures cause a whistling sound and Eddie is going to
think his batteries are running low or that someone has alu-
minum foil in their hair.

And you cannot put someone who eats salt and regular
food next to someone who can't have anything except a
stainless steel fork and water because, if you do, they're not
going to like each other. Somebody who has just had a hip
transplant has to have an outside-at-the-end-of-the-table
seat because they're going to cramp up. Another person has

to be closer to the door because he is carrying nitroglyc-
erin. Another person has to have more light than another
person because his glaucoma is kicking in. And then, of
course, there's a diabetic who doesn't want to sit next to
someone who is overweight, etc., etc. So this is what happens with that. And that's the end of that.

The Day I Decided to Quit Show Business

OR

The Night I Met the Enemy and It Was I

WHEN I PLAYED GREENWICH VILLAGE in the late sixties, I worked at a place called the Gaslight. In fact, not only did I perform at the Gaslight, I *lived* there! In a storage room upstairs above the club. Obviously, at that point my rise to fame hadn't really started yet.

My salary was $100 a week and, believe me, $100 a week did not go a long way, even back then. However, being in my middle twenties, I was hip. And I still had a shot at going back to college and graduating if it didn't work out. So everything was cool. I didn't mind the struggle because I just looked at it as temporary. I could always go back and get my degree.

My job at the Gaslight was described to me by the fellow who hired me. His name was Dave.

"Your job," Dave told me, "is to break up the monotony of the folk singers."

But the truth was, we had some great, great singers there who were not monotonous. They were about as far from boring as you can get.

Tom Paxton played the Gaslight.

Buffy St. Marie.

Lynn Chandler. One night, Lynn pointed to a guy—a white fellow sitting in the back—who used to come in once in awhile. Not often, but enough to know he was there. He was a friend of Lynn's and Lynn said that his name was Bob Dylan and that he was going to be something. So I said to myself: "Right!"

Hal Waters. Hal's wife used to make his suits. Right there, while Hal was singing.

Alex Dobkin, a young lady from Temple—she was at the Ambler Campus, an art major—worked at the Gaslight. She was a folk singer. Played guitar. We were both very, very proud that two people from Temple worked at the club.

Across from the Gaslight was a club called the Fat Black Pussycat. I don't remember exactly why, but the name had something to do with W. C. Fields. Either he went there or he said "fat black pussycat" in a movie or used to go to another place named the Fat Black Pussycat or he called somebody a fat black pussycat. Whatever. The place became associated with W. C. Fields.

I once saw Hugh Romney at the Fat Black Pussycat. Hugh was a storyteller and he liked to talk about cows in

Denver. He became quite a celebrity in that area—Greenwich Village. And Tiny Tim sang at the Fat Black Pussycat.

Catty-corner from the Gaslight was Cafe Wha. The star comedian was Richard Pryor.

Down the street, at Bleecker and MacDougal was the Cafe Figuero.

Greenwich Village was really something then. Peter, Paul, and Mary were always walking up and down the street and the place was loaded with students from all the colleges around. On weekends, everybody came in from maybe five, six states to drop in on Greenwich Village. This was at the end of the heyday, though, because right after this, LSD and all kinds of other pills came in. These drugs got to some of the kids who lived one story above all the chaos. And, sad to say, some of those kids became addicted.

A short time after I started working there, the Gaslight changed hands. Dave sold the place to fellow by the name of Clarence Hood. Clarence Hood was an elderly gentleman, must have been in his late sixties. He was from Mississippi, a white man, about five foot nine, I guess. And he always wore a topcoat—this salt and pepper, herringbone topcoat—even in the summertime!

Well, it took me awhile to get used to that Mississippi drawl, twang, whatever you want to call it. All I know was, when he spoke in that accent, it made my shoulders go up to my earlobes and all of my nervous system said: "Watch it!"

Mr. Hood was very, very close friends with a black man by the name of Mississippi John Hurt, who also worked the Gaslight. Mississippi John Hurt had this very tender, soft voice and he played the twelve-string guitar. I liked to listen to him, listen to his soft voice mispronounce words. But he mispronounced words in a Mississippi way and I liked that.

Anyway, Mr. Hood was probably one of the top people I met during that era.

One night, as usual, I went to the Gaslight to do my at least five shows a night. This fellow came in and sat up front. I didn't know who he was, I thought he was just a customer. So I did my act—about twenty-five minutes—and I was funny. After the show, Mr. Hood introduced me to him and I found out his name was Alan Riback and that he owned a club in Chicago called Gate of Horn, which was a folk house.

Mr. Riback had really enjoyed my show so he booked me into the Gate of Horn, where I opened for Oscar Brown, Jr. Also, a group called the Tarriers. I opened for them.

I was making $125 a week, plus they paid my round-trip transportation. I was in Chicago. I had never been in Chicago in my life, so now I was big time! I was staying at the Hotel Maryland for seven dollars a night. Man, I was big time! And I was still going to Temple University.

Big time!

But even though I was big time, I knew I wasn't *big* time. And that's why I kept looking across the street.

At Mr. Kelly's.

Now, Gate of Horn was a very, very nice place. I mean, even though it was a folk room, it was very hip and very nice and I was very proud to work there. But across the street was a really big-time club.

Mr. Kelly's.

You see, in those days, there were a whole bunch of clubs across the country—like Basin Street East at Forty-ninth and Lexington in New York, or the Hungry Eye in San Francisco—which were *the* spots. They were on the same level as Mr. Kelly's. And the level of the guys who played at these clubs was very high. They were making huge money. Huge—$2,500 a week! Out of this world!

I was making $125. These guys were making $2,500. They were on Ed Sullivan and they were on TV—I had not been on TV.

Guys like Lenny Bruce, Dick Gregory, Jackie Leonard, Mort Sahl, Jonathan Winters. Jonathan was king! Shelly Berman. Elaine May and Mike Nichols probably worked there. George Kirby might have worked there too, although I'm not sure. The point is, these clubs were the pinnacle. The top. You knew you had made it when you worked one of these places. Once you played there, I mean, you were *big* time.

Meanwhile, there I was playing the Gate of Horn. And I stared across the street and often wondered: *Gee whiz man, will I ever get to play Mr. Kelly's?*

I finished my run at the Gate of Horn and went back to

New York, back to the Gaslight. (I don't know what it was with these gates and gasses but I was playing these places. Gaslight, Gate of Horn.)

Back in New York, I got an agent—I joined the William Morris Agency. Things were going really well for me. And then one day it got even better. I got the call. *The* call. From my agent. And he told me he had gotten an offer for me to play Mr. Kelly's.

Mr. Kelly's!

Opening act at $350 a week—$350 a week! I had never made that much money in my life!

So, they flew me to Chicago and I got myself a suite at the Hotel Maryland for twelve dollars a day and then I went to Mr. Kelly's and put my clothes in the dressing room.

Brothers George and Oscar Marianthal owned Mr. Kelly's. I'm not sure if they were twins but they looked a lot alike. Anyway, they had seen me somewhere, I don't know where, and they obviously liked me because they booked me.

So, I was sitting in my dressing room in Mr. Kelly's, a small dressing room, and it was somewhere around two o'clock, and my mind started to tell me that I wasn't really funny enough to be in a club like Mr. Kelly's. I was sitting there and every so often I'd get these flashes.

Flash! *You are not funny*.

And the feeling would come that I wasn't that funny. It

would go away—I would *make* it go away—but certainly from two o'clock on, until the first show, which was at eight o'clock, well, all during those six hours I began, without moving my lips, to talk myself into the *fact* that I was not funny and I really and truly had no business playing Mr. Kelly's.

These performers. They are on TV. They have proven themselves. And you? You are just a Temple University student and I don't know what you think you are doing, but you certainly have no business in front of this crowd, which is a hard-liquor crowd. These people have seen the best and they're going to not see the best tonight.

And so I beat myself down to a point of not believing I was funny and just knowing that I was going to not do well because I knew that I was not funny.

But I went downstairs anyway.

I had a sport coat on, slacks, tie. I looked good. I looked like a professional comedian. And then the fellow introduced me: "Ladies and Gentlemen, Mr. Kelly's is proud to present one of the fastest rising new comedians, Mr. Bill Cosby!"

And there I was. Onstage.

At Mr. Kelly's.

I forget who the headliner was, I really can't remember, but it was about half a house. Let's say the place held 250 people, and there were about a hundred people there and half of them, maybe sixty people, applauded.

Anyway, I did my act, which was supposed to be a twenty-five minute act, I did it in twelve minutes. Twenty-five minutes of comedy in twelve minutes.

There was no laughter.

Of course, I left no *time* for laughter. And certainly, while I was talking, those poor people in the audience didn't see anything funny because what I did was I gave a speech. They were my routines but I delivered them like a *speech* and I did it in twelve minutes. And then I said: "Thank you very much and good night."

I waved at them and the same people who clapped me onto the stage did not clap me off.

I went up to the dressing room and I had this horrible feeling—not that I wanted to throw up—but I had this horrible feeling that this was it. This was the end of my career. And I talked to myself again without moving my lips and I tried to make myself feel better.

Okay, and you've had a good time, but you certainly are not funny and you don't want to do this again. You don't ever want to do this again because it's a horrible, horrible feeling.

As a matter of fact, it was the first time I had ever felt that way.

So, I was sitting in the dressing room and there was a knock on the door and the door opened and there was George Marianthal—no Oscar, just George. George came in and he closed the door. I had both arms across my chest and I was bent over and I never looked up. I just said to Mr.

Marianthal: "Mr. Marianthal, I am very, very sorry for what happened and I am very sorry for what I did tonight. I refuse to accept any pay from you."

"Good," Mr. Marianthal said. " 'Cause you stink!"

"And as soon as I get the money, I will pay you back for the plane trip, the hotel room, and everything else, but I will not be going out to do the second show. I am going back to Temple University."

"I think you should."

"I am going to play football and I am going to graduate from college and get my master's and my doctorate."

"Exactly!"

"So, thank you very, very much for this opportunity, Mr. Marianthal. And I really apologize to you, but I will *not* be going back out on that stage."

"Good," Mr. Marianthal said. "You are not going back out on that stage because you, sir, are not good."

I felt terrible. Just terrible. But Mr. Marianthal didn't let up.

"You, sir, embarrassed me," he continued. "You embarrassed my brother. And even though you embarrassed us, let me say that you don't have to pay us back one iota. You owe us nothing, sir. Just take your things with you and you may leave."

Mr. Marianthal started for the door. He stopped and turned back around to face me.

"Will you do me a favor?" Mr. Marianthal asked.

"Sure," I said. Of course, I would have done anything to feel less terrible, to somehow make amends.

"When you get back to your hotel," Mr. Marianthal said, "will you tell Bill Cosby to come back here and do the second show and to never again send you because, sir, you are *not* funny. Bill Cosby is very, very funny. I don't know why he sent you. Probably because he was afraid. Who knows what happens in the minds of entertainers? But sir, *you* get out of here and you bring Bill Cosby, you *send* Bill Cosby, do whatever, but Bill Cosby *has* to come back here and do the second show."

I looked at Mr. Marianthal. He looked at me. And then he went on: "And you tell Bill Cosby that if he doesn't come back, my brother and I are going to sue him for whatever it is he has. I don't care if it's the sport jacket or those loafers you have on, I don't know. I don't know who owns those clothes but if you *have* to, give Bill Cosby those clothes and have him put them on. You go to the Hotel Maryland and you get Bill Cosby and come back here. No, you have Bill Cosby come back here for the eleven o'clock show. Don't *you* show up. *You* go home!"

Mr. Marianthal opened the door, gave me a look and said with emphasis: "Now *you* get out. And don't forget, I want Bill Cosby back here."

I went back to the hotel.

Despite what Mr. Marianthal had tried to do, it didn't

lift my spirits. I didn't feel any better. I sat in the room wondering what I was going to do. And I just knew that the man was going to sue me. But that didn't make any sense. I had no money and he couldn't sue my parents. If he wanted the sport coat I had, he wasn't going to get anything from that.

So I went back to the club.

I was embarrassed when I walked through the door and I was hoping that the same people who had seen me earlier were not there. I just walked straight through the club—no sense of pride, no reason to feel any pride, and nobody said anything to me. A trio was playing some hip kind of jazz music and the place seemed to have a few more people than the first show.

So I went up to the dressing room and I just sat there. Nobody came in. The flowers that came with a note from the Marianthals welcoming me to Mr. Kelly's were still there—they hadn't taken them away. So I just sat there and I didn't feel any better.

Show time!

I came downstairs and I stood there. Two minutes to eleven. The trio stopped and the people politely applauded and I stood in the dark ready to go on for this horrible, horrible punishment. Standing in front of these people who had seen the best and the greatest and now they were going to see the worst.

Eleven o'clock.

The announcer said: "Ladies and Gentlemen . . . Bill Cosby."

Just that. Bill Cosby. No fastest-rising. Nothing. And that introduction took me out of whatever self-pity I was wallowing in because it hurt.

Ladies and Gentlemen . . . Bill Cosby.

Bill Cosby? And I knew that I was better than that. *Whaddayoumean Bill Cosby? What happened?*

And I shouted as I was walking on the stage.

"What happened to the part—you just said Bill Cosby— what happened to the part . . ."

And the people began to chuckle because they thought it was part of the routine because I said: "What? When you introduced me in the first show, you said I was one of the fastest rising young, fastest rising new comics. And now this time, you just say Bill Cosby?"

And the announcer, I don't remember, I don't know who the fellow was, he said: "That's because I saw the first show."

And the place broke up.

Now, ordinarily, I guess this would have meant destruction for a performer. But for me, well, it just took me out of the self-degradation and all of that. And I began to talk to the guy.

"Well," I said. "I'll tell you something, it *was* a terrible show."

And then Bill Cosby—the Bill Cosby in me—came out and I did about ten minutes on my behavior and the twelve-minute show that I did. I didn't say anything about Mr. Marianthal because I really didn't know the man but I looked in the back and I couldn't find him. I was hoping he was watching.

So, I did twenty-five minutes and I think I only did about seven minutes of prepared, written material. The applause was wonderful. And I left the stage, headed up to my dressing room, and my arms were not folded across my chest. I just sat there, rather relieved, but not completely. I still had some feelings, some self-doubt.

Okay, okay. But there's tomorrow. Do I have to wait until eleven o'clock when they're drunk?

And there was a knock on the door. It was Mr. Marianthal. George. And he came into the dressing room.

"Bill, wonderful show," he said. "Who was that horrible fellow you sent for the first show?"

And I looked up at him and I said: "Mr. Marianthal, I hope to never send him out on the stage again."

And Mr. Marianthal said: "If you do, you ought to really, before you even think about it, realize that there are some people out there who want to laugh."

The Lone Ranger

MOST OF YOU ARE NOT OLD ENOUGH to understand the tremendous blow many people my age suffered by the recent passing of Clayton Moore. The Lone Ranger. He was one of my heroes. Every time one of these people—Dizzy Gillespie, Miles Davis, Clayton Moore—when they die, that means I am going to die. There's no doubt about it. I am going to die.

Hi, ho, Silver! Away!

I think the Lone Ranger added the word *away* after the program first started on radio. He had to say *away* because you couldn't see him. I remember, in the beginning the Lone Ranger would just yell: "Hi, ho, Silver." But then a lot of people listening to the radio wrote in and said: "What?" So the writers had to add the word *away* and then the people knew the Lone Ranger meant for Silver to take off. (The only thing I don't understand is that when the Lone

Ranger came on television, and you could see him, why didn't he stop saying *away*?)

So, I said to a fellow—Jonathan Winters: "Jonathan. What do you think? The Lone Ranger died."

And Jonathan said: "Yeah. Too bad."

And I said: "What happened to Tonto? Is Jay Silverheels gone?"

"Oh, yes," Jonathan told me. "Jay left before Clayton."

We reflected for a moment about the passing of Clayton Moore. And then Jonathan said: "The Lone Ranger and Tonto. That was some racist stuff going on."

"What do you mean?" I asked.

"Well," Jonathan said, "you know what *Tonto* means, don't you?"

I didn't.

"*Tonto* means stupid," Jonathan said.

I said: "What?"

And he said: "Oh, yeah. *Tonto* is a Spanish word that means stupid."

So, I hung up with Jonathan. I was perplexed. I'm remembering when I was running up and down in the neighborhood and if I couldn't be the Lone Ranger, the next person I wanted to be was Tonto. That's right. There I was running around the projects playing Lone Ranger and Tonto with my friends. And if I couldn't be the Lone Ranger, then I had to be what?

Stupid.

And there were many days I *fought* people to become Stupid.

Nobody ever said: "Well, *Tonto* means stupid."

Not on the radio. I never read it in the news. And nobody in the neighborhood ever said anything about *Tonto* meaning stupid. Of course, we didn't have any Spanish-speaking people in the projects yet. The projects I moved into were built in 1944, and there were no Spanish-speaking people. We were African American and Protestant. We didn't have any Spanish-speaking people and we didn't have any Catholics. It wasn't until 1947 that a family from Puerto Rico moved in. This was a culture shock for us because they spoke Spanish. And they were Catholic. So we looked at them really strange. And what added to the stress was the fact that their nine-year-old son's name was spelled J-E-S-U-S.

I remember one day, while I was going to the store—and you had to leave the projects to go to the store—that about nine or ten winos, and I mean *winos*, of all colors, had circled poor Jesus. And these winos were all looking at Jesus and they were pointing to a bucket of water and they kept pointing to it. There was a lot of tension there. Oh, yes, he was in deep trouble.

Okay. The Lone Ranger called Tonto Tonto. What did Tonto call the Lone Ranger?

Kemosabe.

K-E-M-O-S-A-B-E. But what does *Kemosabe* mean? I didn't know. So I decided to do some research.

There is no word *Kemosabe* in Spanish. So I wondered if it was a Native-American word. But no matter what tribe I spoke to, they didn't have the word *Kemosabe*. It just didn't exist. So, if there was no K-E-M-O-S-A-B-E in the Native-American language, nor a K-E-M-O-S-A-B-E in Spanish, what could it possibly mean?

(A lot of people think *Kemosabe* means "My dear friend." *Right!* Here was the Lone Ranger saying "stupid" and Tonto was saying "my dear friend." I don't think so.)

Anyway, a Spanish fellow told me that there was a word in Spanish: *sabe*, which means "to know." But what about *kemo*?

Now, this all was before chemotherapy, so I figured that *kemo* didn't mean "chemical." But maybe, I thought, if I started doing some work in a sounds-like way, I might come up with an answer. Kemo—Key-mo. What does "key" sound like?

Quien. A Spanish word that is pronounced Key-en and means "who." Aha! I was getting somewhere!

Key—who. *Sabe*—know.

I thought about this for a while and finally I said to myself: *What about the* mo? *What rhymes with the* mo *in Ke-mo-sabe?*

The word *no.*

So now I had come up with *Ke-no-sabe.* Translation: Who no know.

And suddenly, there it was! *Who no know*. Or, to extrapolate it further: *Who knows nothing*.

It now seemed clear to me that Tonto, in Spanish, was calling the Lone Ranger: "He who knows nothing."

So I wondered how scarred a sixty-three-year-old man can be after finding out that his heroes—Tonto and Kemosabe—were really Stupid and He Who Knows Nothing. And I told this to my wife (I was very depressed) and my wife looked at me and she said: "They sound like a married couple."

LOGIC CUTS OUT LONG CONVERSATION.